CAMPAIGN 409

HAMBURGER HILL 1969

Operation *Apache Snow* in the A Shau Valley

JAMES H. WILLBANKS   ILLUSTRATED BY RAMIRO BUJEIRO

OSPREY PUBLISHING
Bloomsbury Publishing Plc
Kemp House, Chawley Park, Cumnor Hill, Oxford OX2 9PH, UK
29 Earlsfort Terrace, Dublin 2, Ireland
1385 Broadway, 5th Floor, New York, NY 10018, USA
E-mail: info@ospreypublishing.com
www.ospreypublishing.com

OSPREY is a trademark of Osprey Publishing Ltd

First published in Great Britain in 2024

© Osprey Publishing Ltd, 2024

All rights reserved. No part of this publication may be reproduced or transmitted in any form or by any means, electronic or mechanical, including photocopying, recording, or any information storage or retrieval system, without prior permission in writing from the publishers.

A catalog record for this book is available from the British Library.

ISBN: PB 9781472861535; eBook 9781472861559; ePDF 9781472861542; XML 9781472861566

24 25 26 27 28 10 9 8 7 6 5 4 3 2 1

Maps by Bounford.com
3D BEV by Paul Kime
Index by Richard Munro
Typeset by PDQ Digital Media Solutions, Bungay, UK
Printed by Repro India Ltd.

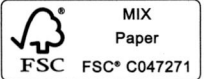

Artist's note

Readers may care to note that the original paintings from which the color plates in this book were prepared are available for private sale. All reproduction copyright whatsoever is retained by the publishers. The artist can be contacted at the following email address:

ramirobujeiro@yahoo.com.ar

The publishers regret that they can enter into no correspondence upon this matter.

Osprey Publishing supports the Woodland Trust, the UK's leading woodland conservation charity.

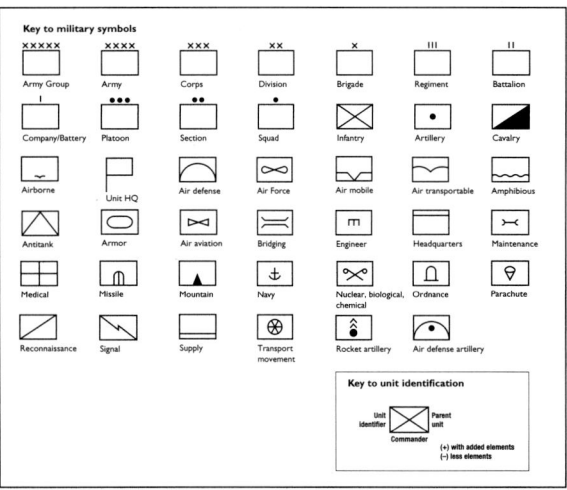

To find out more about our authors and books visit www.ospreypublishing.com. Here you will find extracts, author interviews, details of forthcoming events and the option to sign up for our newsletter.

Unit abbreviations

US company, battalion, and regiment names frequently appear in abbreviated form throughout this work. A/1/1st Marines, for example, refers to A Company, 1st Battalion, 1st Marine Regiment; 2/7th Cavalry refers to 2nd Battalion, 7th Cavalry Regiment, and so on.

Front cover main illustration: Initial combat assault by allied forces into the A Shau Valley, May 10, 1969. (Ramiro Bujeiro)
Title page photograph: US soldiers inspect the damage in the surrounding area of Dong Ap Bia in the aftermath of the battle. (United States Army Center of Military History)

CONTENTS

ORIGINS OF THE CAMPAIGN 5
The A Shau Valley . Precursors to Operation *Apache Snow*

CHRONOLOGY 14

OPPOSING COMMANDERS 17
Allied . North Vietnamese Army

OPPOSING FORCES 24
Allied . Communist . Orders of battle, Operation *Apache Snow*

OPPOSING PLANS 33
Allied plans . NVA plans

THE CAMPAIGN 37
Day 1 . Day 2 . Day 3 . Day 4 . Day 5 . Days 6–7 . Day 8 . Day 9 . Day 10 . Final assault

AFTERMATH 88

THE BATTLEFIELD TODAY 92

FURTHER READING 94

INDEX 95

ORIGINS OF THE CAMPAIGN

The bloody ten-day battle of Hamburger Hill in 1969, part of Operation *Apache Snow*, is considered one of the most controversial battles of the Vietnam War. Although US and South Vietnamese forces were ultimately successful in taking the hill, the battle caused a furor in Congress, led many Americans to question the wisdom and utility of continuing the war, and helped convince the Nixon administration to adopt a new strategy in Vietnam.

The United States had been involved in Vietnam since 1950. During the First Indochina War between France and the Viet Minh, the US provided equipment and advisers to France in a proxy war against the spread of communism in Southeast Asia. When the Viet Minh defeated the French at the battle of Dien Bien Phu in 1954, and the country was subsequently divided at the Geneva peace conference, the United States chose to support the fledgling South Vietnamese government against Ho Chi Minh and North Vietnam.

Initially, the United States focused on the advisory effort to build, equip, and train the Republic of Vietnam's armed forces. However, US ground troops were deployed to South Vietnam in March 1965. The initial contingent of US Marines was followed by a rapid build-up of US armed forces in-country, and the war rapidly expanded in scope.

By the beginning of 1969, with more than a half-million American troops on the ground, US involvement in Southeast Asia had reached a pivotal point. The Communist forces had been defeated decisively on the battlefield during the 1968 Tet Offensive, but they had reaped a tremendous psychological victory in the process. Although US troop levels were at an all-time high and much had been said about the "light at the end of the tunnel," the sheer scope and ferocity of the Communist attacks during the early months of 1968 had been stunning, and the cries to get out of Vietnam reached a new intensity. A shaken President Lyndon Johnson announced that he would not run for re-election. Hubert Humphrey and Richard Nixon squared off in a fight for the soon-to-be-vacated White House.

During his campaign, Nixon made the war in Vietnam a major element of his platform, promising "new leadership that will end the war and win the peace in the Pacific." He proclaimed, "The nation's objective should be to help the South Vietnamese fight the war and not fight it for them ... If they do not assume the majority of the burden in their own defense, they cannot be saved." Despite his later protestations to the contrary, such pronouncements gave many voters the impression that Nixon had a "secret plan" for ending the war, which no doubt was a factor in his victory at the polls in November.

President Richard Nixon meets with US troops stationed in Vietnam during a 1969 tour of the war zone. (Corbis/Getty Images)

General Creighton Abrams succeeded General William Westmoreland as commander of US Military Assistance Command, Vietnam, on June 10, 1968. (PhotoQuest/Getty Images)

On January 20, 1969, Richard Milhous Nixon took the oath of office as the 37th president of the United States. Once elected, Nixon faced the same problems in Vietnam that had confronted Lyndon Johnson. Escalation and commitment of increased numbers of American troops had not worked; the Tet Offensive had demonstrated that fact only too clearly. The resultant stalemate was unacceptable, not only for those clamoring for a US pull-out, but also for an ever-increasing sector of the American people who had initially supported the war but would no longer tolerate a long-term commitment to what appeared to be an unwinnable war. The only answer was to get out of Vietnam. However, the problem was devising an exit strategy that would enable the United States to withdraw gracefully without abandoning South Vietnam to the Communists.

The new president faced a serious dilemma. He had promised to end the war and bring the troops home. Still, Nixon could not, as Henry Kissinger later observed in his memoir, "simply walk away from an entire enterprise involving two administrations, five allied countries, and thirty-one thousand dead as if we were switching a television channel." Nixon had to devise an exit strategy to get the United States out of Vietnam without "simply walk[ing] away." While the survival of South Vietnam remained an objective, it manifestly was not the prime goal, which was to get American troops out of Vietnam. Nixon and his advisers began to consider how the US could disengage itself from the conflict while giving the South Vietnamese a reasonable chance of survival after the American departure. They acknowledged that this would be difficult and might prove impossible in the long run.

While the Nixon administration debated the way ahead, the war continued in Vietnam. In June of 1968, General William C. Westmoreland, who had commanded US Military Assistance Command, Vietnam (MACV) since January 1964, departed for Washington, DC, where he became the Army Chief of Staff. He was succeeded at MACV by his former deputy, Creighton W. Abrams, Jr. Some historians have asserted that General Abrams instituted a new strategy in the war, but that was not true, at least initially. Abrams essentially continued Westmoreland's strategy of taking the war to the enemy. He charged his commanders to maintain "unrelenting pressure on the VC/NVA [Viet Cong/North Vietnamese Army] main force units." He added, "We must carry the fight to the enemy and complete his destruction." As one MACV officer recounted, Abrams initially focused on "aggressive preemptive operations by attacking the enemy in his base camps and dislodging his logistical system." Operation *Apache Snow* and the battle for the A Shau Valley were part of this strategy.

THE A SHAU VALLEY

The A Shau Valley had long played a vital role in the Vietnam War. It is located in far western Thua Thien Province, about 65km west of the coastal city of Hue. In 1969, Thua Thien (today known as Thua Thien Hue Province) was the second-northernmost province in the Republic of Vietnam. It was bordered to the north by Quang Tri Province, to the east by the South China Sea, to the south by Quang Nam Province, and to the west by the Kingdom of Laos.

The A Shau Valley runs from southeast to northwest for 45km. It is flanked by two densely wooded mountain ridges whose summits vary in elevation from 900m to 1,800m. Across the northern end of the valley runs the Da Krong River. Route 548, a loose-surface, dry-weather road, runs almost the entire length of the valley.

Just beyond the ridges to the west lies the aforementioned Laotian border. By this point in the war, the A Shau had long provided a key infiltration corridor for Communist forces and supplies from the Ho Chi Minh Trail in Laos to the coastal cities of the northern I Corps Tactical Zone (I Corps or I CTZ). An NVA presence in the valley posed a threat, not only to Hue, but also to South Vietnam's second-largest city, Da Nang, in Quang Nam Province on the coast.

Just across Laos's border from the valley's north end, Base Area 611 provided an important NVA staging and logistics area. At the opposite end of the valley, in a salient of Laos that abutted Thua Thien to the north and Quang Nam to the south, lay Base Area 607. This area served as a transshipment point for troops and supplies moving into South Vietnam. Both base areas were connected with the A Shau by a complex of well-camouflaged roads and trails protected by anti-aircraft weapons and counter-reconnaissance teams.

The A Shau Valley had extremely inhospitable terrain, characterized by a jumble of ridges, low mountains, gorges, and other steep terrain, which made any attempt at ground maneuver a lengthy, exhaustive process. It was dominated at its northern end by Dong Ap Bia (Ap Bia Mountain), or as the local Pacoh Montagnard tribesmen called it, the "mountain of the crouching beast." Designated

Aerial view of Dong Ap Bia in May 1969 showing smoke from the battle. (Archive Image/Alamy Stock Photo)

A contemporary view of Dong Ap Bia and the surrounding A Shau Valley. (Nigel Killeen via Getty Images)

A Shau Valley, 1969

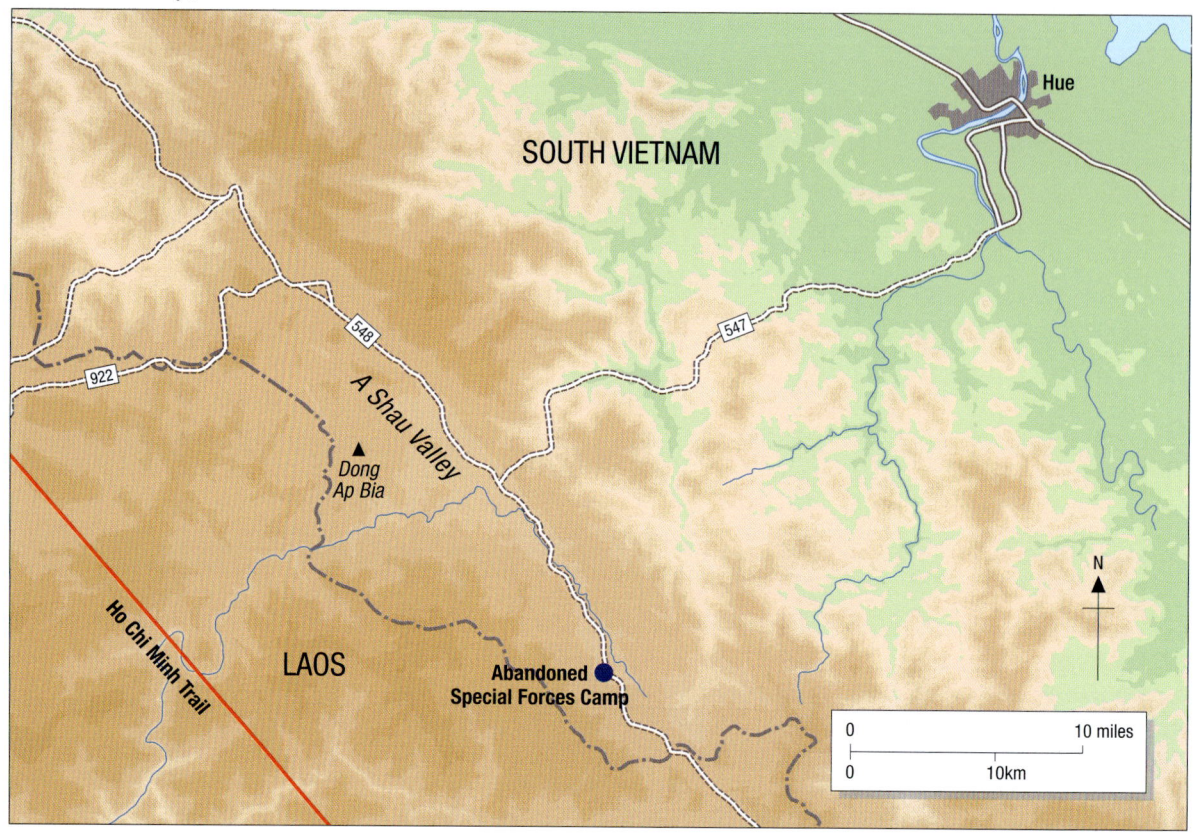

Hill 937 on the map for its height in meters, several prominent ridges and fingers ran out from its summit, one of the largest extending southwest to a height of 900m and another reaching south to a 916m peak. The mountain and associated peaks occupied an area over 2km from north to south and 3km east to west. It was characterized by steep slopes, heavy undergrowth of sawtooth elephant grass, thick stands of almost impenetrable bamboo, and double- and triple-canopy jungle, which rose to 60m in height in some places. It was bordered on the west by the Trung Pham River and the Laotian border, on the north by Dong So Ridge, and on the south by the Rao Lao River.

Because the A Shau Valley, including Dong Ap Bia, had long been a major logistics center for the NVA, the army had fortified the area with bunkers, spider holes, trenches, deep tunnels, and underground storage facilities. The surrounding terrain and thick rainforest vegetation made aerial reconnaissance difficult and complicated close air support. For these reasons, the valley had harbored NVA units that could quickly infiltrate the surrounding areas and attack allied forces and installations in the region.

Regarding weather, the A Shau suffered from the worst of the northeast and southwest monsoons. Consequently, either low overcast, fog, or heavy rain dominated the weather pattern in the area. During the months of May to November, the area was subject to heavy rains, which made trafficability in the area very difficult. Additionally, the poor weather conditions often degraded visibility and hampered air operations during the rainy season.

PRECURSORS TO OPERATION *APACHE SNOW*

Because of its long-standing important role in support of North Vietnamese operations against the coastal provinces and key cities in the northern region, the A Shau Valley had drawn the attention of allied planners since the earliest days of American involvement in the war. In March 1963, a US Army Special Forces (SF) team headed by Captain Jerome Bruschette and a mobile strike force of the Civilian Irregular Defense Group (CIDG) established a camp in the valley to monitor VC activity in the region. Over the next three years, several SF teams rotated in and out of the camp. The Americans focused on training the indigenous CIDG strikers, while conducting reconnaissance patrols and continually improving the base. They were harassed and sniped at constantly; several Americans were killed in the sporadic contacts, mostly ambushes, during this period, but there were no large-scale NVA attacks.

That changed in early 1966 when there was increasing evidence that the NVA was starting a build-up in the A Shau, and it seemed that an assault on the camp was highly probable. The Americans and their 200 strikers made preparations for a major attack. It came on March 9 when, at 0400hrs, the 95th Regiment from the 325th Division launched a heavy mortar barrage that lasted for two and a half hours, killing or wounding over 50 defenders. Following the bombardment, two NVA companies attacked the camp. However, the defenders turned the attack back without further friendly casualties. During the day, the Americans attempted to use close air support against the NVA attackers, but the cloudy weather hampered visibility and, thus, degraded the effectiveness of the airstrikes. The camp, however, did receive several aerial drops of supplies and were able to evacuate some of the wounded by helicopter.

At 0400hrs on March 10, the NVA again began to shell the camp heavily. At 0500hrs, they launched a ground attack. During the battle, one of the striker companies abandoned their positions and joined the attackers, opening a wide gap in the camp's defenses. The fighting soon degenerated into hand-to-hand combat as the Americans and the CIDG troops that remained loyal were pressed into a smaller and smaller area.

At 1500hrs, III Marine Amphibious Force (III MAF), senior US military headquarters in I Corps Tactical Zone, decided to evacuate the remaining camp survivors. At 1700hrs, a Marine helicopter force attempted a rescue, but, in the process, two Marine CH-34s were shot down. Only about 70 strikers were evacuated before the aerial rescue attempt was called off.

A flight of Hueys approaches a landing zone in the A Shau Valley. (Bettmann/Getty Images)

At 1800hrs, approximately 100 camp survivors, including seven Green Berets and the crews of the two downed helicopters, attempted to escape and evade to the north. Most of them made it to a safe area and were rescued on March 11 or 12. Of a total camp population of over 400 troops, only 186 escaped, including 12 Americans, all of whom were wounded. Five US soldiers did not survive the battle.

The fall of the SF camp effectively secured undisputed control of the entire valley for the North Vietnamese forces for several years. There were several allied attempts after the SF camp fell to confront the North Vietnamese in the valley. However, the A Shau effectively became an "economy of force" zone, and subsequent allied forays into the valley were limited in nature and they did not achieve any lasting change to the NVA control of the area.

In 1967, "Project Delta" long-range reconnaissance patrols began probing the A Shau. Although limited in size and scope, these patrols provided good intelligence on NVA activity in the area. The North Vietnamese responded with counter-reconnaissance units, resulting in a series of small but sharp battles. Even though the recon patrols located several huge NVA supply dumps, MACV opted not to follow up at that time other than to bomb the area with B-52s. Several allied operations targeting the A Shau were planned later in 1967, but as the NVA threat against Khe Sanh (a Marine combat base farther to the northwest in Quang Tri Province near the Laotian border) developed in the latter months of the year, these plans were shelved. This allowed the North Vietnamese and Viet Cong to use the valley as they saw fit, and it would figure prominently when the Tet Offensive of 1968 began.

Soldiers from the 1st Cavalry Division move up a road constructed by the combat engineers in the A Shau Valley as part of Operation *Delaware* in April 1968. (Bettmann/Getty Images)

As the North Vietnamese made preparations for the general offensive to coincide with the Tet holiday in January 1968, their forces used the valley to stage the attacks in the northern region of South Vietnam. Ten battalions of Viet Cong and North Vietnamese troops transited the valley en route to attack the ancient capital city of Hue. On January 31, those forces launched the attack and captured the city, occupying and holding it for 25 days.

After a bloody three-week battle, US Marines and South Vietnamese forces retook the city. After Hue returned to allied control, a counterattack was mounted into the A Shau Valley in April by the US 1st Cavalry Division (Airmobile), the Army of the Republic of Vietnam (ARVN) 1st Division, and an ARVN airborne task force. Called Operation *Delaware/Lam Son 216*, it was the first significant assault on the A Shau Valley in four years. During the operation, which began on April 19 and ended on May 17, 1968, the US and ARVN forces reported more than 800 NVA killed in action and the destruction of several supply dumps, including 134,000 rounds of small-arms ammunition, thousands of artillery shells, and several heavy weapons. However, upon completion of the operation, the allied forces, who sustained 142 killed in action, were airlifted out by helicopter, enabling the North Vietnamese forces to move back into the area.

By early July 1968, intelligence gained from aerial reconnaissance and long-range recon patrols indicated that the North Vietnamese had reoccupied the A Shau Valley. There were reports of new truck parks, roads, storage depots, and defensive positions. This build-up in the valley resulted in a plan to send allied troops back into the area to address the new threat.

On August 4, 1968, two battalions from the 1st Brigade of the 101st Airborne Division and two ARVN battalions plus the elite ARVN Hac Bao (Black Panther) Reconnaissance Company from the 1st ARVN Division launched Operation *Somerset Plain*. The operation began with an airmobile assault from Firebase Birmingham into the valley near A Luoi to disrupt the NVA logistics network and forestall any new attacks into I Corps. The allies initially encountered only scattered NVA supply caches and made only light contact. However, on the night of August 10/11, NVA forces from the 816th and 818th Main Force Battalions attacked the ARVN 3rd Battalion, 1st Infantry Regiment. The ARVN called in close air and artillery support, and the North Vietnamese troops withdrew after sustaining several dozen men killed in the fighting. Total allied losses for the operation included seven US and 14 ARVN killed,

Members of 2/327th Infantry, 101st Airborne Division, make their way across a river in the A Shau Valley during Operation *Somerset Plain* in August 1968. (US Army/Getty Images)

US Marines fire 105mm howitzers into the A Shau Valley in support of their fellow Marines as part of Operation *Dewey Canyon* in February 1969. (Bettmann/Getty Images)

Elite South Vietnamese Hac Bao (Black Panther) troops from the 1st ARVN Division are inserted by UH-1H Huey during a combat assault in the A Shau Valley. (Bettmann/Getty Images)

Troopers from the 101st Airborne Division conduct reconnaissance in force after being inserted into the A Shau Valley by a flight of Hueys as part of Operation *Massachusetts Striker* in March 1969. (Bettmann/Getty Images)

including eight South Vietnamese soldiers who died when a US artillery round fell short. On August 17, the allied forces began to withdraw from the valley by helicopter.

During the latter months of 1968, allied efforts in the A Shau Valley again focused on interdiction from the air. Initially, airstrike availability was limited due to the southwest monsoon adversely affecting flying conditions. This situation changed as the monsoon season came to an end. Additionally, when President Johnson announced a bombing halt of North Vietnam on November 1, 1968, more assets became available for striking targets in the south, including those in the A Shau Valley.

Despite the air interdiction efforts, aerial observers noted intensifying NVA activity in the valley and the adjoining area in Laos. It became clear that the NVA was initiating a new build-up in the valley. Therefore, General Creighton Abrams, commander of US MACV, wanted to target the A Shau. He hoped to destroy the NVA in the area and prevent it from launching new attacks from Laos through the valley toward Hue and Da Nang. Accordingly, a series of operations were initiated beginning early in 1969.

On January 22, three battalions of the 9th Marines, 3rd Marine Division, launched Operation *Dewey Canyon* into the northern end of the A Shau in the Da Krong area. During the two-month operation, the Marines established several firebases and landing zones, sweeping the area of operations for enemy forces and supply caches. As the Marines advanced, they found that the NVA had constructed major roads in the area, and intelligence revealed that as many as 1,000 trucks were moving supplies into base camps in the area. The Marines even discovered an eight-building field hospital fully equipped with Soviet-made surgical instruments, medicines, and other medical supplies.

Ultimately advancing to the Laotian border, the Marines captured 16 122mm guns, 73 anti-aircraft guns, 92 trucks, and more than 525 tons of weapons and supplies, including nearly 1,000 AK-47s and over a million rounds of small-arms and machine-gun ammunition. This represented the single largest NVA weapons cache captured in the war to that date.

As the Marines neared the border, the encounters with the North Vietnamese picked up in intensity. Ambushes and platoon-sized fights erupted throughout the area. In the fighting that ensued, including a limited Marine incursion across the border into Laos, the Marines reported over 1,600 North Vietnamese killed in action while losing 130 of their own. The operation officially ended on March 19, and the Marines were helicoptered out of the valley.

By the time *Dewey Canyon* concluded, it was clear that this new NVA build-up in the A Shau posed a significant threat to Hue, Quang Tri, and the other major cities and towns in the I Corps Tactical Zone. Accordingly, Lieutenant General Richard G. Stilwell, commander of XXIV Corps, ordered a new campaign to eliminate the North Vietnamese forces in the area. This campaign would include three phases, with the second phase being Operation *Apache Snow*.

The first phase was Operation *Massachusetts Striker*, launched by the 2nd Brigade of the 101st Airborne Division and the 3rd Regiment of the 1st ARVN Division into the valley's southern end. The operation aimed to interdict Route 548 at the Laotian border, block any NVA forces trying to escape into Laos, and sweep the area to find and destroy enemy forces, supply caches, and lines of communication.

The operation began on March 1, 1969 with the establishment of Firebase Whip, which would serve as 2nd Brigade's forward command post (CP) for *Massachusetts Striker*. With the CP established, 1st Battalion, 502nd Infantry air assaulted into an area southwest of abandoned Firebase Veghel. Additional allied forces, including the 2/501st and 3/3rd ARVN, were brought in by helicopter and began to conduct sweep operations in their assigned areas of operation.

During *Massachusetts Striker*, the US and South Vietnamese troops uncovered massive North Vietnamese supply depots and pushed the NVA forces to the north, fighting several pitched battles near Dong A Tay, which became known as "Bloody Ridge." The North Vietnamese put up a dogged defense of the area, losing over half of a nearly 700-man battalion either killed or wounded in the 33-day fight. The Americans lost 35 killed and more than 100 wounded. This battle would prove to be a harbinger of worse things to come.

With the southern A Shau Valley more or less secured, the second operation, *Apache Snow*, focused on the northern portion of the valley. This operation was a continuation of the effort to keep the North Vietnamese forces in the A Shau off balance and to prevent them from using the valley as a staging area for an attack on Hue and the coastal provinces. A third operation, Operation *Montgomery Rendezvous*, was planned as a follow-up to *Apache Snow*, focusing on the eastern and central part of the A Shau Valley floor.

CHRONOLOGY

1966

March 9–11   Viet Cong troops overrun US Special Forces camp at A Shau near the Laotian border after two days of savage fighting.

1968

April 19 to May 17   1st Cavalry Division and elements of the 1st ARVN Division along with a South Vietnamese airborne task force conduct Operation *Delaware* in the A Shau Valley to preempt enemy preparations for another attack on the Hue area.

August 4–20   1st Brigade, 101st Airborne, and elements of 1st ARVN Division conducted Operation *Somerset Plain* in the A Shau Valley to destroy NVA supplies and cut enemy lines of communication.

1969

January 22 to March 18   Three battalions of the 9th Marines (Reinforced), 3rd Marine Division, conduct Operation *Dewey Canyon* north of the A Shau and Da Krong valleys in Quang Tri and Thua Thien provinces to disrupt enemy base areas threatening Hue.

February 28 to May 6   2nd Brigade of the 101st Airborne Division and 3rd Regiment of the 1st ARVN Division conduct Operation *Massachusetts Striker* in the southern end of the A Shau Valley to destroy NVA forces, supply caches, and lines of communication.

April 25 to May 9   Air Force C-130s "prep" 30 possible landing zones in the A Shau Valley with 15,000lb "Daisy Cutter" bombs to confuse the NVA about the actual landing zones to be used in Operation *Apache Snow*.

May 7–9   1st and 2nd Battalions, 9th Marines, are inserted into the southern end of Da Krong Valley to block NVA escape routes into Laos in support of Operation *Apache Snow*.

May 10   After more than an hour of artillery fire and close air support, Operation *Apache Snow* begins when 65 Huey helicopters insert three battalions from 101st and two ARVN battalions into the north end of the A Shau Valley. 3/187th lands near Dong Ap Bia and begins the assault on the mountain.

May 11   3/187th advance is halted after its CP is hit by friendly fire from two Cobra gunships leaving two dead and wounding another 35.

May 12   3/187th companies re-position and prepare for a new coordinated attack.

May 13	In the early morning hours, NVA sappers and elements of an NVA battalion attack Firebase Airborne; the defenders beat back the attack, but sustain 22 killed and 61 wounded in the fighting.

A US aircraft drops a bomb too close to B Company, 3/187th, killing one man and wounding another.

A helicopter attempting to evacuate wounded from D Company, 3/187th, is shot down, resulting in six killed in action. |
May 14	3/187th renews attack up Ap Bia; 12 are killed and 80 wounded in the fighting; friendly fire from a helicopter gunship kills one soldier and wounds three more in B Company.
May 15	B Company, 3/187th, gets to within 150m of the summit when helicopter friendly fire hits the CP, killing two, wounding 14, and forces the company to pull back to its previous position.
May 16	1/506th attacks and takes Hill 916, but is stopped 2km from Hill 937's summit.
May 17	3/187th awaits the arrival of the 1/506th and prepares for the next assault on Hill 937.
May 18	3/187th attacks from the north; 1/506th attacks from the south; artillery prep including CS gas shells begins 30 minutes late; CS gas drifts over friendly troops, especially those of A Company, 3/187th.

D Company, 3/187th, is stopped just short of Hill 937 summit, and suffers 50 percent casualties, with every officer killed or wounded.

C Company, 3/187th, is stopped by a rainstorm and forced to withdraw.

General Zais considers calling off the operation because of heavy casualties and heightened media attention, but decides to commit three additional battalions.

By this date, A and B Companies of 3/187th have suffered 50 percent losses; C and D Companies have suffered 80 percent losses.

Associated Press correspondent Jay Sharbutt's report on the fight for Hill 937 appears in US newspapers. |
| May 20 | Ten artillery battalions hit the top of Hill 937 with 20,000 rounds, and 272 airstrikes drop over a million pounds of bombs and 152,000lb of napalm.

3/187th, reinforced with a company from 2/506th and 2/3rd ARVN, capture Hill 937.

On the floor of the US Senate, Senator Edward Kennedy calls the attack on Dong Ap Bia "senseless and irresponsible ... madness." |

May 21	3/187th flies to Eagle Beach for R&R via Firebase Blaze; General Zais defends the attack on Hamburger Hill at a news conference.
May 23	General William Westmoreland, Army Chief of Staff and former MACV commander, privately congratulates Zais "on a gallant operation … which I refuse to recognize as the much-publicized Hamburger Hill." President Nixon's press secretary reiterates that the assault was consistent with the administration's "tactics and military strategy."
May 24	*The New York Times* reports that some Nixon administration officials fear such costly battles will undermine public support for the war; Senator Kennedy calls the battle nothing but "cruelty and savagery," and Senator George McGovern denounces the "senseless slaughter."
May 29	Senator Stephen Young compares the battle for Hamburger Hill to the American Civil War's battle of Chancellorsville.
June 5	Major General John Wright, who had succeeded Major General Zais as commanding general of the 101st Airborne Division, orders allied forces to abandon Dong Ap Bia.
June 8	President Nixon confers with South Vietnamese President Nguyen Van Thieu at Midway Island and announces plans to "Vietnamize" the war and to begin troop withdrawals of 25,000 by July 8, and 35,000 more by early December.
June 17	The press reports that the NVA is again on Dong Ap Bia in force, and US intelligence admits that some 1,000 NVA have reoccupied the hill. General Wright tells reporters that if it becomes necessary to take Hamburger Hill again, he is prepared to commit "everything it takes, up to the entire division, to do the job."
June 19	Senator Young criticizes both Wright and Zais for being "so callous over the welfare of GIs who do the fighting and dying." President Nixon orders General Creighton Abrams to "conduct war with a minimum of American casualties."
June 27	*Life* magazine runs photos of 242 Americans killed in Vietnam in one week.
July 7	US troops from 3rd Battalion, 60th Infantry Regiment, 9th Infantry Division depart South Vietnam as the first increment of 15 subsequent troop withdrawals under President Nixon's Vietnamization policy that will continue through early 1973.
August 15	The Nixon administration issues a new mission statement for MACV that centers on assisting South Vietnamese armed forces "to take over an increasing share of combat operations" as US forces continue their withdrawal.

OPPOSING COMMANDERS

ALLIED

American

The commanding general of XXIV Corps during Operation *Apache Snow* was **Lieutenant General Richard G. Stilwell**. He was born in 1917 in Buffalo, New York. Stilwell attended Brown University before graduating from the United States Military Academy at West Point in 1938 with a commission in the Corps of Engineers.

During World War II, Stilwell took part in the Normandy invasion. He served briefly under General George Patton after the war during the occupation of Germany. From there, he became a special military adviser to the US Embassy in Rome before moving on to the Central Intelligence Agency.

During the Korean War, Stilwell commanded the 15th Infantry Regiment in the 3rd Infantry Division and then served as senior adviser to the Republic of Korea (ROK) Army I Corps. After the armistice in Korea, he was promoted to brigadier general and served as the Commandant of Cadets at West Point.

From 1965 to 1967, Stilwell commanded US Military Assistance Command, Thailand (MACTHAI). From there, he went to Fort Hood, where he commanded the 1st Armored Division. In 1968, he was posted to Vietnam, where he initially served as deputy commanding general of III Marine Amphibious Force, and then assumed command of XXIV Corps.

After the Vietnam War, he served as Deputy Chief of Staff for US Military Operations at the Pentagon from 1969 to 1972. After that assignment, he took command of the Sixth US Army at the Presidio of San Francisco in 1972–73. In 1974, he became Commander-in-Chief of the United Nations Command in Korea. After retiring from the Army in 1981, Stilwell served as US Deputy Undersecretary of Defense for Policy until 1985. He died on December 25, 1991, in Falls Church, Virginia.

The commanding general of the 101st Airborne Division (Airmobile) in the spring of 1969 was **Major General Melvin Zais**. He was born in Fall River, Massachusetts, on May 8, 1916. Zais attended Louisiana State

Lieutenant General Richard G. Stilwell (right), seen here with General Andrew Goodpaster (left) in August 1968, was commanding general of XXIV Corps during Operation *Apache Snow*. (US Army Signal Corps photo, US National Archives)

University as a journalism major before transferring to the University of New Hampshire, where he graduated with a Bachelor of Arts degree in political science in 1937. That year he was commissioned a second lieutenant in the US Army Reserve.

In 1940, Zais joined the original parachute infantry battalion, which would eventually be expanded to become the 501st Parachute Infantry Regiment. During World War II, he was commander of the 3rd Battalion of the 501st Parachute Infantry Regiment and, later, served as the executive officer of the 517th Parachute Infantry Regiment. He saw action in Italy, southern France, and the Battle of the Bulge.

Zais was promoted to brigadier general on June 1, 1964. In 1966, he was the assistant division commander of the 1st Infantry Division in Vietnam. Returning to the States, Zais served as the Director of Individual Training, Deputy Chief of Staff for Personnel in the Pentagon. Again posted to Vietnam in 1968, he assumed command of the 101st Airborne Division (Airmobile). He was promoted to lieutenant general on August 1, 1969, and became the commanding general of XXIV Corps later that year.

After returning from Vietnam in 1970, Zais served as Director of Operations, J-3, Joint Chiefs of Staff in the Pentagon. He commanded Third US Army from 1972 to 1973. That year he was promoted to four stars and appointed Commander of Allied Land Forces South-Eastern Europe. He held that position until his retirement on May 31, 1976. He died in Beaufort, South Carolina, on May 5, 1981.

Major General John M. Wright replaced General Zais as commander of the 101st Airborne Division (Airmobile) shortly after the culmination of Operation *Apache Snow*. This change had been scheduled for some time and was not connected with the outcome of the operation.

Wright was born on April 14, 1916, in Los Angeles, California. Upon graduating from the United States Military Academy in 1940, Lieutenant Wright was assigned to the 91st Coast Artillery on Corregidor, an element of the harbor defenses of Manila. During the battle for Corregidor, he was captured by the Japanese and spent three and a half years as a prisoner of war. He survived the sinking of the Ōryoku Maru, which was transporting Wright

Major General Melvin Zais was the commanding general of the 101st Airborne Division (Airmobile) during Operation *Apache Snow*. (Terry Fincher/Hulton Archive/Getty Images)

US artillerymen prepare to fire in support of Operation *Apache Snow* on May 10, 1969. (ENNIO IACOBUCCI/AFP/Getty Images)

and his fellow POWs to Japan. Wright was liberated in September 1945. He later wrote about his experiences in his book *Captured on Corregidor: Diary of an American POW in World War II*.

After a year of hospitalization to recover from his captivity, he transferred to the infantry and qualified as a parachutist. During the Korean War, Lieutenant Colonel Wright served in the 7th Infantry Division as 32nd Infantry Regiment executive officer, Division G-1, and Division G-4. After returning from Korea, he earned a master's degree in business administration and attended the National War College.

After several assignments in Germany, Wright was promoted to brigadier general and became assistant division commander of the 11th Air Assault Division (Test). When the division was reflagged as the 1st Cavalry Division, Wright led the advance party that departed for Vietnam in August 1965 to establish the division's base of operation there in preparation for the arrival of the rest of the division. After returning from Vietnam, he was promoted to major general and served on the Army Staff. In 1967, he became Commanding General of the Infantry Center and Commandant of the Infantry School at Fort Benning, Georgia.

In 1969, Major General Wright returned to Vietnam. He assumed command of the 101st Airborne Division (Airmobile) from Major General Zais and held that position until May 1970. After returning from Vietnam, he was promoted to lieutenant general and appointed Comptroller of the Army, his last duty assignment before retiring in 1972. After retirement, Wright held various high-level positions as an administrator in the Boy Scouts of America. He died in Riverside, California, on January 27, 2014 at the age of 97.

The commander of the 3rd Brigade of the 101st Airborne Division (Airmobile) during Operation *Apache Snow* was **Colonel Joseph B. Conmy, Jr**. The son of an Army officer, Conmy was born at Fort Snelling, Minnesota, on March 12, 1919. He grew up on various Army posts in the continental US, the Philippines, and Hawaii and graduated from Leilehua High School in Hawaii in 1937. Conmy attended the United States Military Academy, graduating in 1943 with a commission as a second lieutenant in the infantry. In World War II, he served as a platoon leader and company commander in

Europe with the 114th Infantry Regiment. In the Korean War, he commanded a company and then a battalion in the 7th Infantry Division.

After the Korean War, Conmy served as an instructor in tactics at West Point and attended the Command and General Staff College and the Army War College. From 1956 to 1959, he was assigned to NATO headquarters in Paris. In 1962, Conmy took command of the 3rd Infantry Regiment, "The Old Guard," at Fort Meyer, Virginia. Later in the 1960s, Colonel Conmy was a military aide to President Lyndon B. Johnson, traveling extensively with the president.

In 1968, Conmy went to Vietnam to command the 3rd Brigade of the 101st Airborne Division (Airmobile). He returned to the US in 1969 and retired from the Army in 1973. After retiring, he became a research engineer for several companies. Conmy died of cancer at his home in Vienna, Virginia, on April 22, 1994.

Lieutenant Colonel Weldon F. Honeycutt was the commander of the 3rd Battalion, 187th Infantry Regiment, during the battle for Dong Ap Bia in 1969. Honeycutt was born in 1931 and grew up in a large family in the mill town of Greensboro, North Carolina, during the Depression. He joined the Army in 1946 at 16, having lied about his age. After completing basic training, he was assigned to the 82nd Airborne Division. In 1951, he attended Infantry Officer Candidate School at Fort Benning, Georgia, and was commissioned an infantry second lieutenant upon graduation in November of that year.

During the Korean War, he commanded a rifle company in the 187th Airborne Regimental Combat Team, commanded by then Colonel William C. Westmoreland. When two companies in the 187th failed to take a key hill from the Chinese during a fight along the 38th Parallel, Honeycutt led a third assault, overran the hill, and drove off the Chinese. Westmoreland was impressed with Honeycutt's aggressiveness and courage, nicknaming him "Tiger," a name that stuck for the rest of his career.

After returning to the States, he was selected for flight school, where he learned to fly both fixed-wing and rotary-wing aircraft. In 1958, he

Lieutenant Colonel Weldon Honeycutt gives orders to his company commanders as their units work their way up the slopes of Dong Ap Bia. (Hugh Van Es/Associated Press/Alamy Stock Photo)

Paratroopers marshal for upcoming Operation *Apache Snow*. (Bettmann/Getty Images)

was assigned to the 101st Airborne Division at Fort Campbell, Kentucky, where he served as aide-de-camp to his commander from Korea, William Westmoreland, by then a major general.

Early in the Vietnam War, he assembled a special helicopter task force and was influential in the development of helicopter-borne tactics. After attending the Command and General Staff College at Fort Leavenworth, Kansas, he returned to Vietnam. Initially assigned to the 1st Cavalry Division, he requested reassignment to the 101st Airborne Division (Airmobile). Slotted originally for an aviation unit, he assumed command of the 3rd Battalion, 187th Infantry Regiment, in January of 1969. The unit was known as the "Rakkasans," a World War II nickname for paratroopers, roughly meaning the "umbrella guys" in Japanese.

When he took over the battalion, he found that many of the unit's officers were not in the field and were hanging around Camp Evans. He ordered every officer back into the field, except those essential in the rear. He announced, "From now on this battalion is gonna fight. This battalion is gonna go out and find the enemy and kill him. This bullshit of running around and hiding is over."

Honeycutt was a profane, hot-tempered, and aggressive commander who nevertheless won the grudging respect of many of his soldiers with his drive, toughness, and professionalism. Abrasive, Honeycutt seemed to thrive on controversy and revel in the intense feelings he engendered in others.

During the battle of Hamburger Hill, he gained the nickname "Blackjack" after his radio call sign. He was immensely proud of his unit and its soldiers, constantly urging them to live up to the high standards he expected of them. During the battle for Hamburger Hill, many of his soldiers complained about Honeycutt, but most of them later, free of the heat of the action, agreed that his leadership had won the battle. Lieutenant Frank Boccia, whose own hot-tempered personality often clashed with that of Honeycutt, wrote after the war that the lieutenant colonel was "harsh, brutal, egocentric, and demanding," a man who "was impossible to like." Despite that characterization, Boccia said he "was a helluva fighting soldier" who "was the paradigm of a battlefield commander." Honeycutt retired as a brigadier general in 1980 after 34 years of service.

Major General Ngo Quang Truong was commanding general of the 1st ARVN Division in 1966–70. (Bettmann/Getty Images)

The other US Army battalions that took part in the battle for Dong Ap Bia were the 1st Battalion, 502nd Infantry Regiment, commanded by Lieutenant Colonel Donald Davis; 2nd Battalion, 501st Infantry Regiment, commanded by Lieutenant Colonel Joseph C. Wilson; 1st Battalion, 506th Infantry Regiment, commanded by Lieutenant Colonel James Bowers; and 2nd Squadron, 17th Cavalry Regiment, commanded by Lieutenant Colonel William W. DeLoach.

Also participating in the battle in the A Shau Valley were two Marine battalions from the 9th Marine Regiment. Lieutenant Colonel Thomas J. Culkin commanded the 1st Battalion and Lieutenant Colonel George C. Fox commanded the 2nd Battalion.

South Vietnamese

The senior South Vietnamese commander in the northern region was **Lieutenant General Hoang Xuan Lam**, commander of I Corps. Lam and I Corps would not play a significant role in the conduct of Operation *Apache Snow*. However, his 1st ARVN Division provided several battalions for the operation under the control of the 101st Airborne Division.

The commander of the 1st ARVN Division was **Major General Ngo Quang Truong**. Truong was considered one of the most honest and capable generals in the South Vietnamese Army. Ngo Quang Truong was born on December 19, 1929, to a well-to-do family in the Mekong Delta province of Kien Hoa. After he graduated from My Tho College, Truong attended the reserve officer school at Thu Duc and was commissioned as an infantry officer in the South Vietnamese Army in 1954. During the course of his career, which was spent primarily in airborne units, Truong built a reputation as a charismatic leader who led from the front and took care of his soldiers.

In 1966, when violent civil disorders broke out in Central Vietnam by Buddhists protesting military control of the government, Truong, then a colonel, was appointed as acting commander of the 1st Infantry Division in Hue. Truong, as a Buddhist, was uncomfortable commanding a unit charged with quelling the Buddhist demonstrations, but he carried out his duties with his usual professionalism and Saigon subsequently made the appointment permanent. With his brand of hands-on leadership, Truong quickly molded the division, which did not have a very good reputation prior to his arrival, into one of the best units in the South Vietnamese Army.

During Operation *Apache Snow*, several battalions, primarily from the 1st Regiment of Truong's division, would operate alongside US troops. The commander of the 1st Regiment, 1st ARVN Division, was Colonel Phan Van Hoa. The commander of the 2nd Battalion, 3rd Regiment, was **Lieutenant Colonel Pham Van Dinh**. Dinh and his battalion would play a significant role in the battle for Dong Ap Bia.

Pham Van Dinh was born on February 2, 1937, in Phu Cam village in Thua Thien Province. He was born into a middle-class urban family, all of whom were practicing Catholics. He attended the prestigious Pellerin School, a Catholic school in Hue city. Then he attended the Thu Duc Reserve Officers School outside Saigon and, upon completion, was commissioned as a second lieutenant in the infantry. Dinh was a good leader with a stellar reputation; he rose quickly through the ranks. In February 1967, he assumed command of the 2nd Battalion, 3rd Regiment, of the 1st Division.

Dinh served with distinction, including participation in the fight for Dong Ap Bia, until 1972. In April of that year, Dinh was commanding the 54th Regiment of the 3rd ARVN Division in the northern I Corps Tactical Zone. The NVA launched its Eastertide Offensive on March 30, pouring across the Demilitarized Zone (DMZ) in massive numbers. In the ensuing battle, Dinh's regiment, which was defending Camp Carroll, was surrounded and pummeled by North Vietnamese artillery. Feeling isolated and abandoned by his superiors, Dinh surrendered with all his officers and men to the Communists, who promised him that his men could rejoin their families. Several months later, Dinh agreed to join the NVA, on the condition that he would never have to fight his former comrades. All of this could not have been foreseen in May 1969 as his unit prepared to take part in Operation *Apache Snow*.

NORTH VIETNAMESE ARMY

Senior Colonel Chu Phuong Doi was the commander of the 324th Division at the time of the battle for Dong Ap Bia. A member of the Tay ethnic minority group, he was born in 1922 in Hung Dao village, Hoa An District, in Cao Bang Province in northern Vietnam. He joined the Viet Minh in 1946, and during the First Indochina War against France, Chu Phuong Doi rose from platoon commander to deputy regimental commander and fought in many campaigns, including the 1954 battle of Dien Bien Phu. During the war against the Americans, he commanded the 316th Brigade fighting in northern Laos from 1961 to 1962. In March 1965, he became deputy commander of the 324th Division. During March 1967–68, he served as commander of three different divisions in succession (the 325th, the 169th, and the 324th) in the Tri Thien Military Region.

From 1972 to 1973, Chu Phuong Doi served as deputy commander of the Tri Thien Military Region. From 1978 to 1981, he was the deputy commander of the Vietnamese Volunteer Army Forces in Laos. He was promoted to major general in 1980, and the following year, he assumed command of the Vietnamese forces in Laos and continued in that assignment until 1987.

The 29th Regiment was commanded by **Colonel Ma Vinh Lan**. His subordinate battalion commanders included Tang Van Mieu of the 7th Battalion, Dinh Xuan Bai of the 8th Battalion, and Nguyen Minh of the 9th Battalion. Very little is known about the brigade and battalion commanders of the 29th Regiment. The NVA operated under a dual-command system down to the company level, with a political commissar taking part in the decision-making process at each level. One can reasonably assume that the brigade and battalion commanders in the 29th Regiment probably had been fighting for several years, were very experienced, combat-hardened, well-prepared, and, accompanied by their political commissar, were highly motivated ideologically for the coming fight in the A Shau Valley.

OPPOSING FORCES

ALLIED

US forces

By the summer of 1969, all US forces in South Vietnam were under the command of MACV. By this point in the war, there were more than half a million American soldiers, Marines, airmen, sailors, and coastguardsmen in-country.

For command and control purposes, the South Vietnamese Joint General Staff had divided Vietnam into four areas, designated Corps Tactical Zones (CTZ), numbered I, II, III, and IV from north to south. Although this arrangement had been established by the South Vietnamese Joint General Staff, MACV adapted its command and control arrangements to this structure. There was no consolidated combined headquarters, and the Americans and South Vietnamese had their own separate parallel chains of command.

The I CTZ consisted of five provinces and was the northernmost military region in South Vietnam. The two most northern provinces in the area, Quang Tri and Thua Thien, were bordered on the north by the DMZ, on the south by Quang Nam Province, on the east by the South China Sea, and on the west by the Laotian border. A narrow coastal plain characterized the area, but most of the terrain to the west of the coast was dominated by hills and the Annamite Mountain chain.

Before 1968, the senior US headquarters in I CTZ was the III Marine Amphibious Force (III MAF), which had been initially formed in 1965 to command the Marine Corps units committed in the region. At the beginning of 1968, III MAF, a corps-level command, controlled more than 100,000 Marines, sailors, and soldiers.

The Marine Corps divisions subordinate to III MAF were the 1st and 3rd Divisions, plus 3,000 Marines from the 7th Fleet's two special landing forces attached to III MAF. The Marine ground units were supported by the 1st Marine Air Wing based in southern I Corps. In addition to the Marine Divisions and Air Wing, in early 1968, III MAF also controlled the Army's 1st Cavalry (Airmobile), 23rd Infantry (Americal), and 101st Airborne Divisions plus the 3rd Brigade from 82nd Airborne Division.

During the 1968 Tet Offensive, there were major attacks in I Corps, including those at Khe Sanh, Quang Tri, and Hue. During the heavy fighting that marked the offensive, the controlling and planning capability of III MAF headquarters was severely taxed by the presence of the additional Army forces. Accordingly, General Westmoreland established MACV Forward headquarters in the Hue–Phu Bai area on February 9, 1968 to assist in stemming the tide of the North Vietnamese invasion in I Corps. General Creighton Abrams, then deputy commander of MACV, exercised control over all joint combat and logistical forces – Army, Navy, Air Force, and Marine – deployed in the corps area of responsibility.

In March 1968, MACV Forward, having served its purpose, was converted to a corps headquarters and designated Provisional Corps, Vietnam, under the command of Lieutenant General William B. Rosson. Rosson exercised operational control over the 3rd Marine Division (Reinforced), the 1st Cavalry Division (Airmobile), the 101st Airborne Division (Airmobile) (-) (Reinforced), and other assigned corps troops.

On August 15, 1968, the Provisional Corps, Vietnam, was redesignated XXIV Corps and placed under the operational control of III MAF. In late 1968, General Rosson was succeeded by Lieutenant General Richard G. Stilwell as commander of XXIV Corps. Stilwell was responsible for the activities of US Army ground combat units deployed in northern South Vietnam. From his headquarters at Phu Bai, he would exercise command and control over the elements of the 101st Airborne Division (Airmobile) and supporting forces that would fight in the A Shau Valley as part of Operation *Apache Snow*.

The 101st Airborne Division ("The Screaming Eagles") had a long and storied history dating back to World War II. It was activated on August 15, 1942 at Camp Claiborne, Louisiana, and sent overseas on September 5, 1943. The division participated in D-Day, June 6, 1944, parachuting behind enemy lines in the Utah Beach area of Normandy. During the rest of the war, the division jumped into Holland during Operation *Market-Garden* and attacked into the Ardennes Forest to blunt the German counterattack in what became known as the Battle of the Bulge. After the Bulge, the 101st continued its advance toward the Ruhr pocket, reaching Hitler's retreat home at Berchtesgaden at the war's end.

During the years following the end of World War II, the division went through several reorganizations and was involved in a number of missions. It was inactivated and reactivated several times as the Army went through several phases of reorganization, ultimately ending up stationed at Fort Campbell, Kentucky.

The 1st Brigade of the 101st deployed to Vietnam from Fort Campbell, in July of 1965; it was subsequently stationed in the II Corps area. The rest of the division joined the 1st Brigade in 1967. The division was initially redeployed in the III CTZ, although the 1st Brigade continued to operate out of Phan Rang in II Corps. In March of that year, the preponderance of the division was redeployed to the I CTZ. In 1968, the division was taken off jump status and converted to an airmobile division. In April and May 1968, the division participated in operations along the lowlands of Quang Tri and Thua Thien provinces, including the area around Hue.

The 101st Airborne Division (Airmobile) consisted of three infantry brigades made up of ten airmobile infantry battalions, seven artillery battalions, an air cavalry squadron, an aviation group consisting of three assault helicopter battalions, and a division support command.

The airmobile infantry brigade was the largest maneuver element of the division. It was commanded by a colonel and included from two to four battalions, although additional units might be attached for specified operations or periods of time. The brigade also included support from artillery, engineers, air and ground cavalry, and Army aviation.

ARVN soldiers prepare to board helicopters in preparation for combat assault. (US Army/Getty Images)

The controlling headquarters for the battle on Dong Ap Bia was the 3rd Brigade, which consisted of three battalions: 1st Battalion, 506th Infantry; 2nd Battalion, 501st Infantry; and 3rd Battalion, 187th Infantry.

The airmobile infantry battalion was the largest maneuver unit of the airmobile infantry brigade. It was commanded by a lieutenant colonel. The airmobile infantry battalion in 1969 typically consisted of a headquarters company, four rifle companies, and associated supporting arms, including a mortar platoon, a communications element, support and transport elements, and a medical platoon. The battalions deployed to Vietnam in 1967 with three rifle companies, but the battalion headquarters company had been trimmed down to provide the battalion's fourth rifle company.

At the time of the battle for Dong Ap Bia, the infantry battalion headquarters usually consisted of the battalion commander, sergeant major, principal staff officers, and supporting staff personnel. In addition, there were communications and support elements, a medical platoon, and a mortar platoon (armed with four 81mm mortars). These personnel and resources were normally located in or near the forward battalion CP. The battalion executive officer and numerous other personnel from the headquarters remained in the rear to conduct administration and supervise the resupply of the battalion.

The battalion headquarters company consisted of a small field headquarters of about a dozen men, including the company commander, first sergeant, a couple of radio operators, and attached medics. This small element was located near the battalion headquarters. The rest of the headquarters company, including the company executive officer, remained in the rear area to conduct company administration, receive replacements, and push supplies and ammunition forward.

Each rifle company, with an authorized strength of 164 men, had three to four rifle platoons. The platoon was commanded by a lieutenant assisted by his platoon sergeant and a radio operator. Each platoon consisted of three rifle squads and a weapons squad. Each of the rifle squads, which consisted of two fire teams, was led by a squad leader. The rifle squad members were armed with M-16 rifles, except the grenadiers, who were armed with 40mm M-79 grenade launchers.

The weapons squad normally consisted of 11 personnel, including a squad leader, two machine gunners and assistants, two anti-tank gunners and assistants, and two ammo bearers. The machine gunners were armed with M60 machine guns, and the anti-tank gunners were armed with 90mm recoilless rifles. The weapons squad would often be disbanded, and the machine gunners and anti-tank gunners assigned to the rifle squads.

During the battle for Dong Ap Bia, the 3rd Brigade, 101st Airborne, would be supported by elements of the Division Artillery, including one direct support battalion (105mm) and three batteries that provided general support reinforcing fires (105mm and 155mm). Additionally, the brigade could call for fires from any other battalions in the division artillery that were in range, including an aerial rocket artillery battalion equipped with Cobra helicopters.

For airmobile operations, the brigade could call upon the 101st Division Aviation Group, which consisted of three assault helicopter battalions, a general support aviation company, and a heavy helicopter company. These helicopters transported the troops to and from the battlefield and provided aerial resupply and medical evacuation.

For Operation *Apache Snow*, the 101st Airborne Division also had operational control of two Marine infantry battalions from the 9th Marine Regiment and several ARVN battalions from the 1st ARVN Division.

In 1969, a typical Marine infantry regiment included a 222-man headquarters company and three infantry battalions, which were each authorized 1,649 men. Each battalion was organized into four 216-man rifle companies and a 385-man headquarters and service company (H&S). The H&S company included communications, anti-tank, and mortar platoons.

A Marine rifle company included three 47-man rifle platoons. In addition, it had a nine-man headquarters and 66-man weapons platoon that included machine-gun, anti-tank, and light mortar sections.

During Operation *Apache Snow*, the 9th Marine Regiment was supported by artillery fires from the 2nd Battalion, 12th Marines, consisting of three 105mm towed howitzers, two 155mm towed howitzers, and a 107mm mortar battery.

South Vietnamese forces

The Republic of Vietnam Armed Forces (RVNAF), which numbered about 685,000 military personnel in 1969, were controlled by the South Vietnamese Joint General Staff (JGS). South Vietnamese forces included the ARVN, the Vietnamese Air Force (VNAF), the Vietnamese Navy (VNN), and the Vietnamese Marines. The JGS exercised command of the ARVN through four subordinate corps-level headquarters.

North Vietnamese replacements move down the Ho Chi Minh Trail somewhere in Laos in 1968. (AFP/Getty Images)

Each ARVN corps headquarters was responsible for an assigned geographic region (corps tactical zone) and normally had two to three ARVN infantry divisions attached. Additionally, each corps headquarters controlled a number of associated combat, combat support, and combat service support units. These included corps artillery, engineers, signals, logistics, and other elements that supported corps operations.

In addition to the divisions assigned to the four corps headquarters, there were two more divisions that made up the national strategic reserve; these included the Airborne Division and the Marine Division, which were not permanently attached to any corps headquarters and normally responded to orders direct from the JGS.

The senior ARVN headquarters in the area of operations that included the A Shau Valley was I Corps, commanded by Lieutenant General Hoang Xuan Lam. The I Corps area of operation included Quang Tri, Thua Thien, Quang Nam, Quang Tin, and Quang Ngai provinces. To defend this area, Lam had two ARVN divisions under his command – the 1st Division was headquartered in Hue and the 2nd Division was stationed in Quang Ngai Province. Additionally, Lam controlled the 51st Independent Infantry Regiment at Hoi An and the 54th Independent Infantry Regiment at Tam Ky, as well as assorted other forces in his assigned area of responsibility.

Operation *Apache Snow* would be a US-controlled operation conducted by XXIV Corps. However, for the duration of the operation, the 101st Airborne Division had operational control of several battalions from the 1st ARVN Division.

In 1969, the 1st ARVN Division had an authorized strength of 10,450 men. The division was typically composed of three infantry regiments and an artillery regiment of three 105mm howitzer battalions and one 155mm howitzer battalion. The division also included a division headquarters company, an engineer battalion, an armored cavalry squadron, and reconnaissance, signal, transportation, ordnance, quartermaster, medical, and administration companies, plus a military police detachment. The 1st Division, commanded by Major General Ngo Quang Truong, was headquartered in Hue, but its three infantry regiments frequently operated some distance from the division headquarters and often were under the operational control of US headquarters in the I CTZ. This would be the case for Operation *Apache Snow*.

The three infantry regiments of the 1st Division each included four infantry battalions. Each battalion contained a headquarters company and three rifle companies. Each rifle company consisted of three rifle platoons, each with three ten-man rifle squads plus a weapons platoon, which included machine gun, mortar, and rocket-launcher sections. The headquarters company of each regiment had service, medical, transportation and maintenance, mortar and recoilless rifle platoons, and a communication section.

The infantry soldiers in the division's subordinate combat units were equipped with a variety of weapons. The primary weapon for the individual infantryman was the 5.56mm M-16; however, designated soldiers within each infantry platoon were armed with M-60 7.62mm machine guns or M-79 40mm grenade launchers. Additionally, there were also the M18 57mm and M67 90mm recoilless rifles that were also employed by ARVN troops. The standard mortar for the ARVN infantry battalion was the M-2 60mm mortar, but the M29 81mm mortar was also used extensively throughout the infantry division.

In 1969 at the time of the battle in the A Shau Valley, the 1st ARVN Division had a reputation as one of the best divisions in the South Vietnamese armed forces. It was well-trained and well-led. This was not always the case in the ARVN, which was not held in high regard by many American soldiers and Marines.

COMMUNIST

The Communist forces during the battle for Dong Ap Bia included both the *Quan Doi Dang Dan* (People's Army of Vietnam, PAVN) – the regular army of the Democratic Republic of Vietnam, more popularly known by American soldiers during the war as the North Vietnamese Army (NVA) – and, to a lesser extent, the *Quan Doi Giai Phong Nhan Dan* (People's

Liberation Armed Forces, PLAF) – the armed insurgent force in South Vietnam, more popularly known as the Viet Cong (VC).

The lineage of PAVN can be traced back to the armed propaganda groups that fought the Japanese during World War II and evolved into the *Viet Nam Doc Lap Dong Minh Hoi*, or Viet Minh, which fought in the First Indochina War against the French. Following the French defeat at Dien Bien Phu in 1954, the separation of Vietnam and the establishment of the DMZ between the North and South Vietnam, the Viet Minh was organized into a modern fighting force.

The PAVN then evolved into a hybrid organization that included three tiers. At the bottom of the pyramid were the local militia at the district and village levels. At the provincial level, there were regional forces. At the top of the pyramid were Chu Lac, or regular forces, which formed the main conventional troops for both the defense of North Vietnam and the liberation of the South. Over time, weapons and equipment provided by the People's Republic of China, the Soviet Union, and other Warsaw Pact members helped modernize the force.

By the end of 1967, the PAVN had increased to 447,000 men and women, organized into ten infantry divisions, an artillery division, an anti-aircraft division, and over 100 independent regiments. These were conventional military organizations, which were manned, trained, and equipped in North Vietnam and then moved south to take part in the war there.

The *Dang Lao Dong Viet Nam* (Central Committee of the Vietnam Workers' Party) in Hanoi formed and controlled the People's Revolutionary Party (PRP) in South Vietnam. The PRP, in turn, controlled the *Mat Tran Dan Toc Giai Phong Mien Nam Viet Nam* (the National Front for the Liberation of South Vietnam), or, as it was more commonly known, the National Liberation Front (NLF). Established in December 1960, the NLF was both a political organization and an armed insurgent force that exercised control over the VC.

The VC was organized similarly to the PAVN with a triangular arrangement. The apex of the VC organization was the main force units, which were manned by full-time soldiers, many of whom had been trained in the North and infiltrated the South. These forces, also known as territorial or mobile forces, normally operated at the battalion level, but could join to form multi-battalion forces for particular campaigns.

The second rung was the regional or territorial forces. While also full-time soldiers, unlike the main force units, these were primarily composed of locally recruited and trained soldiers who generally operated in the areas where they were recruited. They usually worked as company-sized units but could also join together for particular campaigns.

The last group of VC soldiers was local militia units, which were organized at the village and hamlet levels. These forces were aptly described as "farmers by day and soldiers by night." They operated in groups that ranged from small three-person cells to platoons. Though they could conduct some low-level military operations, they were mostly involved in supporting the regional

Le Duan was secretary of the Lao Dong Party (Working People's Party of Vietnam) in Hanoi and the guiding force behind North Vietnamese strategy in the South. (Sovfoto/Universal Images Group/Getty Images)

NVA soldiers training for combat. (Bettmann/Getty Images)

and main force units and in collecting intelligence, sabotage (including assassination), and other low-level activities.

Under the initial command and control arrangement, the Communists established Military Region V to control NVA and VC operations in I and II Corps (Central Highlands). However, they separated the two northern provinces of Quang Tri and Thua Thien from Military Region V to form a new region, called the Tri–Thien–Hue Front. This region came directly under the North Vietnamese high command, rather than the Central Office of South Vietnam (COSVN), which controlled military operations in the southern two-thirds of the country. The Tri–Thien–Hue Front area of operation included the Hue, Da Nang, and Quang Tri areas, as well as the A Shau Valley.

There could be several NVA divisions in each enemy military region. The divisions were organized and employed for specific operations. They were usually made up of two to four infantry regiments along with various supporting units.

Although still present in the A Shau Valley at the time of Operation *Apache Snow*, the VC had suffered horrendous casualties during the bitter fighting in 1968. The major fighting at Dong Ap Bia, like most of the significant engagements for the rest of the war, was primarily done by the NVA. This was not always apparent, because main-force NVA units often retained traditional VC unit designations. This did not change the fact that these units were manned by regulars who had come down the Ho Chi Minh Trail from North Vietnam.

The controlling NVA division headquarters for the operations in the A Shau Valley at the time of Operation *Apache Snow* was the 324th Division. It was formed in North Vietnam in 1955 by regrouped Southerners from central Vietnam. The 324th was reduced to a brigade in the late 1950s, raised back to division status in 1965, and fought the US Marines in the DMZ area in 1966. After that, the division headquarters was dissolved because its subordinate units were being used only piecemeal as independent regiments, fighting under the direct command of the B5 Front during 1967 and the 1968 Tet Offensive. The 324th Division was re-established in October 1968 with three regiments assigned. The division fell under the command and control of the Tri–Thien–Hue Front.

The regiment from the 324th Division that provided the preponderance of the NVA soldiers who fought in the battle for Dong Ap Bia was the 29th Regiment. Formed in 1965, the regiment was considered one of the NVA's best units, earning the unofficial sobriquet "The Pride of Ho Chi Minh." As a separate regiment, the 29th had fought in Quang Tri Province in 1967 and the battle for Hue during the 1968 Tet Offensive. During the offensive, the regiment had fought very well against the US 1st Cavalry Division in several engagements around the Imperial City. In October 1968, the 29th Regiment became the third regiment of the newly reactivated 324th Division.

In April 1969, the 29th Regiment moved to the Dong Ap Bia area and assumed responsibility for the area of

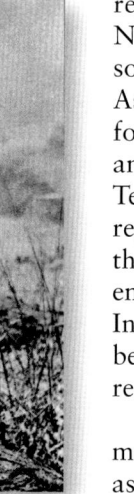

Soldiers of the People's Army of Vietnam (PAVN), also known as the NVA, conducting combat operations in 1968. (Universal History Archive/Getty Images)

FAR LEFT
Ho Chi Minh was the President of the Democratic Republic of Vietnam until his death in September 1969. (Hulton-Deutsch Collection/Corbis/Getty Images)

LEFT
A US soldier reads a letter from home near a pile of NVA B-40 rockets captured along with other weapons during Operation *Apache Snow*. (Bettmann/Getty Images)

operations from the 3rd Battalion, 9th Regiment, which had been defending the area along with elements of the 6th Regiment since the Tet Offensive. Most of the previous defenders, which were understrength and in poor health, were sent to the rear area, most probably in Laos, to rest and receive replacements.

The 29th Regiment consisted of a headquarters, three battalions (7th, 8th, and 9th), two sapper companies, and an engineer company. Infantry regiments in the North Vietnamese Army at full strength usually had about 2,500 troops, but allied estimates put the size of the 29th Regiment when the battle began at between 1,200 and 1,800 men, organized into three infantry battalions.

In addition to the infantry battalions, the 29th Regiment had several supporting units that made up its combat power. There was a mortar company armed with six Type 53 82mm mortars, an anti-aircraft company equipped with up to 18 Type 54 12.7mm DShK heavy machine guns, a recoilless rifle company equipped with six Type 52 75mm recoilless rifles, and a sapper company. In addition to these combat units, signal, engineer, transport, and medical companies were assigned to support the regiment.

The NVA infantry battalion, at full strength, numbered about 550 soldiers. It was usually organized into a headquarters, three rifle companies, and a combat support company. The combat support company, which might be disbanded depending on the manpower needs of the battalion, typically consisted of a 60mm mortar squad and a 57mm recoilless rifle squad. Additionally, the company had three RP-46 general-purpose machine guns that were usually allocated to each platoon.

The NVA rifle companies usually included three rifle platoons, a combat support platoon, and a reconnaissance squad. The rifle platoons consisted of a small headquarters and three rifle squads. There was no standard allocation of weapons, but, usually, the NVA infantrymen were armed with AK-47 assault rifles (or SKS carbines), RPD light machine guns, and RPG-2 or -7 (B-40 or B-41) anti-tank rocket-propelled grenade (RPG) launchers.

The rifle company's combat support platoon was sometimes disbanded, and the personnel reassigned to the rifle platoons. If present, it contained a 60mm mortar squad and a 57mm recoilless rifle squad. Additionally, the company had three general-purpose machine guns that were usually allocated to each rifle platoon.

Fire support for the NVA regiment consisted of a mix of 107mm, 122mm, and 140mm free-flight rockets; 82mm and 120mm mortars; 57mm and 75mm recoilless rifles, and several models of heavy machine guns (like the DShK mentioned above). This weaponry and associated small arms were manufactured by the Soviet Union or were Chinese and North Korean copies of Soviet weapons; ammunition and other war materiel was supplied by the Soviet Union, China, and several Warsaw Pact countries.

The 29th Regiment in the A Shau Valley was well-led, well-trained, and highly motivated. The soldiers were experienced and skilled light infantrymen supported by very effective artillery and mortars. They would prove to be dangerous opponents in the bloody fighting that characterized the battle for Dong Ap Bia.

ORDERS OF BATTLE, OPERATION *APACHE SNOW*

ALLIED FORCES

US forces
XXIV Corps
101st Airborne Division (Airmobile)
   3rd Brigade
      1st Battalion/506th Infantry
      2nd Battalion/501st Infantry
      3rd Battalion/187th Infantry
         A Company/2nd Battalion/506th Infantry OPCON (May 18–21)
      3rd Squadron/5th Cavalry
         D Company/2nd Battalion/506th Infantry OPCON

      Brigade Control
         Brigade Security Platoon
         A Troop/2nd Squadron/17th Cavalry
         2nd Battalion/319th Arty (Direct Support)
         Battery C/2nd Battalion/11th Arty (General Support Reinforcing)
         Battery C/2nd Battalion/94th Arty (General Support Reinforcing)
         Battery C/1st Battalion/83rd Arty (General Support Reinforcing)
         B/326 Engr (Direct Support)
         A/158 Assault Helicopter Battalion
         B/158 Assault Helicopter Battalion
         58th Scout Dog Platoon
         Tactical Air Control Party/20th Tactical Air Support Squadron
9th Marine Regiment
   1st Battalion, 9th Marines
   2nd Battalion, 9th Marines
   2nd Battalion, 12th Marines
      Battery D (105mm, Towed)
      Battery E (105mm, Towed)
      Battery F (105mm, Towed)
      Mortar Battery (107mm)
      2nd Provisional Howitzer Battery (155mm, Towed)
      3rd Provisional Howitzer Battery (155mm, Towed)

ARVN forces
I Corps
1st Infantry Division
   1st Regiment
      1st Battalion
      2nd Battalion
      3rd Battalion
      4th Battalion
      Battery/11th ARVN Artillery (Direct Support)
      Battery/34th ARVN Artillery (General Support Reinforcing)
   3rd Regiment
      1st Battalion
      2nd Battalion
      3rd Battalion
      Battery/12th ARVN Artillery (Direct Support)

NORTH VIETNAMESE ARMY
324th Division
   29th Regiment
      7th Battalion
         1st Company
         2nd Company
         3rd Company
         4th Company
      8th Battalion
         5th Company
         6th Company
         7th Company
         8th Company
      9th Battalion
         9th Company
         10th Company
         11th Company
         12th Company
      16th Signal Company
      20th Sapper Company
      23rd Sapper Company
      Engineer Company
   806th Battalion

OPPOSING PLANS

ALLIED PLANS

Under the overall control of Lieutenant General Richard G. Stilwell's XXIV Corps, elements of the 3rd Marine Division and 101st Airborne Division (Airmobile), in coordination with the 1st ARVN Division, were to conduct Operation *Apache Snow* in the northern A Shau and southern Da Krong valleys to cut NVA supply and infiltration routes at the Laotian border and destroy enemy forces, base camps, and supply caches in the A Shau.

The corps concept of the operation called for the 1st and 2nd Battalions of the 9th Marines to occupy the southern Da Krong Valley to block NVA escape routes into Laos along Route 922. The 101st Airborne Division, in coordination with elements of the 1st ARVN Division, was assigned the primary responsibility for conducting operations to destroy NVA concentrations in the northern end of the A Shau Valley.

Per the corps operational plan, Major General Melvin Zais, commander of the 101st, tasked Colonel Joseph B. Conmy, Jr., and his 3rd Brigade to move into the northern A Shau Valley to seek out and destroy enemy forces there. The 3rd Brigade troops for this operation included its three assigned battalions – 2nd Battalion, 501st Airborne (2/501st), 1st Battalion, 506th Airborne (1/506th), and 3rd Battalion, 187th Airborne (3/187th), plus the brigade had operational control of two battalions from the 1st ARVN Division. The two ARVN battalions would play supporting roles in the operation. At the same time, 3/5th Cavalry, also under Brigade control, would conduct clearing operations along Route 547, where Army engineers were improving the road to provide a route into the heart of the valley.

During the early phase of the operation, 3rd Brigade would be supported by the divisional reconnaissance squadron, 2/17th Cavalry, which would scout landing zones (LZs) and provide gunship support. Additionally, the squadron's aero-rifle platoons, known as "Blues," would serve as a ready reaction force and could be inserted to rescue downed helicopter crews.

Surrounded by barbed wire, spotters watch for enemy movement from a firebase overlooking the A Shau. (Bettmann/Getty Images)

US soldiers go about their duties on a firebase in the northeast portion of the A Shau Valley; five separate firebases provided fire support during Operation *Apache Snow*. (Bettmann/Getty Images)

Apache Snow was conceived as a reconnaissance in force; the intent was to find the enemy and pile on. The assault battalions would assemble approximately 13km east of the A Shau Valley near Firebase Blaze, which would act as a forward supply base for the operation. A multi-battalion airmobile insertion would initiate Operation *Apache Snow* into LZs adjacent to the Laotian border. When one of his units made significant contact with the NVA, Conmy would reinforce it with one of the other units and maneuver his remaining forces to cut off the NVA's retreat and destroy it.

Colonel Conmy suspected that his troops were in for a fight, but he did not have a lot of good intelligence on actual NVA strength or where it was specifically located in the A Shau. The US forces learned some information from captured documents, equipment, and the occasional prisoner, but the NVA was heavily camouflaged and conducted most major movements at night under radio silence and thus had not been detected. Still, Conmy knew that the North Vietnamese were in the area in force and spoiling for a fight; he was eager to oblige them.

D-day was set for May 10. In preparation for the attack, during the period of April 25 to May 9, Air Force C-130s prepped 30 possible LZs in the A Shau Valley with "daisy cutters," 15,000lb BLU-82B bombs, designed to explode just above the ground, clearing away all trees and vegetation without causing a crater. The LZs created by these strikes were scattered randomly across the entire valley to confuse the North Vietnamese about the actual locations of the coming combat assaults.

According to the plan for *Apache Snow*, the American and South Vietnamese troops would be inserted into the valley by helicopter on D-day to disrupt the Communist build-up and destroy NVA forces. Once inserted, the infantry units in their respective areas of operation would be supported by ten artillery batteries firing from five firebases constructed on the high ground east of the valley.

A BLU-82B Commando Vault 15,000lb conventional free-fall weapon is prepared for loading. Known as the "Daisy Cutter," it was dropped from C-130 aircraft to clear helicopter landing zones in Vietnam. (Greg Mathieson/Mai/Getty Images)

NVA PLANS

The battle for Dong Ap Bia would differ from the tactics the NVA and VC customarily used. Ever since the November 1965 battle in the Ia Drang Valley, the first big battle of the war between US and

NVA troops, the NVA and VC had recognized the danger of sustained, conventional engagements with the Americans. US firepower in all its forms – artillery, close air support, and B-52s – was devastating, so the Communists engaged in close-in fights to "grab 'em by the belt" and negate or complicate the Americans' ability to bring their powerful weapons to bear. They usually resorted to surprise attacks or ambushes, where they could withdraw quickly before the Americans' heavy firepower could be directed upon them. When the Americans initiated the attack against NVA positions, they would defend those positions for a short while, then usually withdraw to fight another day.

A giant CH-47 Chinook helicopter brings in supplies to a hilltop firebase in the A Shau Valley. (Bettmann/Getty Images)

Such would not be the case at Dong Ap Bia. The mountain was in a vital area for resupply and reinforcement of Communist troops and sat astride a critical route through the A Shau Valley between Laos and the South Vietnamese coastal area around Da Nang and Hue. It was honeycombed with tunnels and bunkers, providing an excellent place to defend against any American incursions into the area.

According to a unit history published after the war, on the afternoon of May 7, 1969, the 324th Division commander, Chu Phuong Doi, and division political commissar Tran Van An met with Ma Vinh Lan, the commander of the 29th Regiment, and his staff in an expanded planning meeting. Kieu Tam Nguyen, Secretary of the Regimental Party Committee, discussed the

A US Air Force B-52 Stratofortress releases its bomb load over the Vietnam target area, having flown from its base on Guam. (Popperfoto/Getty Images)

General Vo Nguyen Giap was the commander of the People's Army of Vietnam and defense minister; he played a major role in Hanoi's conduct of the war in the South. (Pictures From History/Universal Images Group/Getty Images)

goals and the requirements for the unit in this operation. Then the regimental commander briefed on his plan for the defense of Dong Ap Bia.

The regiment would use its 8th Battalion to defend and hold blocking positions going up the mountain's slopes. It would use the 7th Battalion to conduct mobile operations on the southwestern flanks of Ap Bia. The 9th Battalion would conduct mobile operations on the northern and eastern sides.

The tactical scheme used dug-in fortified blocking positions combined with maneuver attacks involving the entire regiment, making the total annihilation of American troops the primary objective. The plan was to conduct close-quarter battles to intermingle friendly forces with the attackers to limit their use of airstrikes and artillery. The battalions responsible for mobile attacks, the 7th and 9th, would hit the American forces as they arrived in the immediate area surrounding Dong Ap Bia before they launched their assault on the mountain. Meanwhile, the 8th Battalion would continue to strengthen and reinforce its fortifications on the mountain, while training its troops for close-in fighting, particularly the use of claymore mines. Additionally, it would stockpile ammunition, rice, and other combat supplies to enable it to defend and hold its defensive positions on the mountain during a long, multi-day battle.

Division political commissar Tran Van An stressed to all attending the planning meeting that this battle would be an excellent opportunity to kill Americans. He charged his comrades to "make extraordinary efforts, display incredible courage, and use intelligence and creativity in both your attacks and your efforts … to hold the terrain." With that exhortation, the group disbanded and began preparing for the coming battle.

As each side finalized its plans, the stage was set for the intense battle that was to follow. It would be a bloody fight that would last for ten days and ultimately have serious ramifications far beyond the battlefield.

US troops dismount from a Huey helicopter during a combat assault into the A Shau Valley. (Bettmann/Getty Images)

THE CAMPAIGN

DAY 1

On May 10, 1969, with the 1st and 2nd Battalions of the 9th Marines in position and operating out of firebases Razor and Erskine in the southern Da Krong Valley to block NVA escape routes into Laos, 3rd Brigade 101st launched Operation *Apache Snow*. As the infantrymen marshaled at Firebase Blaze and prepared to execute their part of the operation, artillerymen on firebases Bradley, Airborne, Currahee, Cannon, and Berchtesgaden, located along the mountaintops of the eastern A Shau, waited by their guns. At 0600hrs, the artillery began to shell the LZs to be used for this operation. At 0710hrs, the artillery ceased fire and Cobra attack helicopters began to pound each LZ. After the prep fires were concluded, 65 UH-1H Huey helicopters picked up the troops at Firebase Blaze in one of the largest airmobile operations of the war.

The helicopters crossed the valley in the south and then, using the terrain as a screen, turned north along the Laotian border to the selected LZs in the

Forward air controllers flying in OV-10 Bronco aircraft conducted close air support that was so crucial to the US ground forces in the Vietnam War. (USAF Photo via Getty Images)

Paratroops jump from a helicopter during a combat assault into the A Shau Valley as part of Operation *Apache Snow*. (Bettmann/Getty Images)

northern end of the valley where the 1/506th and 3/187th were inserted. The mission of 1/506th, known as the "Currahees," was to interdict routes from the Laotian border to Route 548 in its assigned area. The 3/187th was given the mission of securing Dong Ap Bia.

The third of the four battalions conducting combat assaults in the area of operations was the 2/501st Infantry, which landed at an LZ just east of the Laotian border. The battalion immediately began reconnaissance in force patrols to block NVA infiltration into the valley from Laos. A Company was detached from the battalion to provide security for Firebase Airborne.

Concurrent with the insertion of the US units, the 3rd and 4th Battalions from the 1st ARVN Division were inserted into assigned LZs and began conducting sweep operations northwest of the main objective area. An additional ARVN battalion, 2/1st, joined the operation the following day.

Most of the infantrymen from the 3rd Brigade inserted into the LZs were veterans of other combat assaults, but it was clear to all that this operation was something different. One soldier, John Snyder of B Company, 3/187th, recalled that this was "the biggest movement of troops I have ever experienced and the most helicopters I'd ever seen in one spot … you knew something big was happening, but you didn't know exactly what you were getting into – other than we already knew the A Shau was bad."

Initially, the insertions were unopposed. After landing at its LZ, the 1/506th, including the battalion CP and three rifle companies, first secured the area. Once the LZ was secured, the rifle companies each began their reconnaissance in force along their assigned axes of advance toward the Laotian border as planned.

Meanwhile, Lieutenant Colonel Weldon Honeycutt, commander of the 3/187th Rakkasans, had selected an LZ northwest of Dong Ap Bia on one of its spurs. The battalion began its combat assault into the LZ at 0844hrs. Honeycutt landed along with his D Company. The company immediately began setting up defenses while the battalion CP was being established about 1km from the top of Dong Ap Bia.

Initial insertions, May 10, 1969

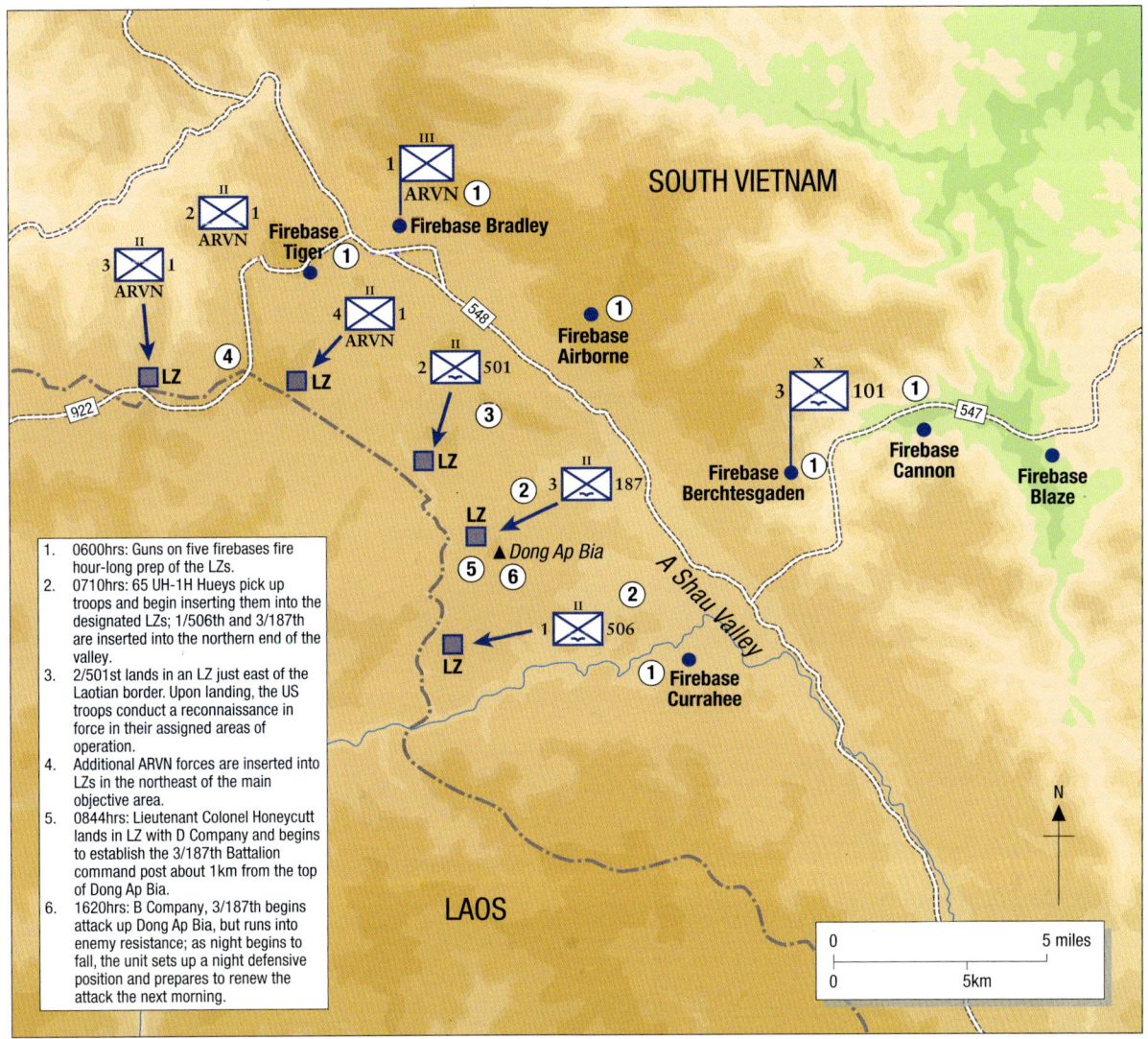

1. 0600hrs: Guns on five firebases fire hour-long prep of the LZs.
2. 0710hrs: 65 UH-1H Hueys pick up troops and begin inserting them into the designated LZs; 1/506th and 3/187th are inserted into the northern end of the valley.
3. 2/501st lands in an LZ just east of the Laotian border. Upon landing, the US troops conduct a reconnaissance in force in their assigned areas of operation.
4. Additional ARVN forces are inserted into LZs in the northeast of the main objective area.
5. 0844hrs: Lieutenant Colonel Honeycutt lands in LZ with D Company and begins to establish the 3/187th Battalion command post about 1km from the top of Dong Ap Bia.
6. 1620hrs: B Company, 3/187th begins attack up Dong Ap Bia, but runs into enemy resistance; as night begins to fall, the unit sets up a night defensive position and prepares to renew the attack the next morning.

As the CP was being set up, Honeycutt directed A Company to move out to the northwest and sent C Company to the southwest to conduct a reconnaissance in force (RIF) in their assigned sectors. As they moved out along their designated routes, they had each proceeded only a few hundred meters when they both discovered NVA huts and bunkers all along their respective lines of advance, some with cooking fires still smoldering, indicating that NVA soldiers had left the area only minutes before the arrival of the American troops.

While the troopers from 3/187th continued to advance, several light observation helicopters (LOHs or "Loaches") from the 2nd Squadron, 17th Cavalry, reported sighting huts and bunkers all over the area around Ap Bia. In mid-afternoon, one of the Loaches flushed half a dozen North Vietnamese soldiers out of a still-occupied position about 2km west of the mountain. The pilot called in Cobra gunships, which took the fleeing troops under fire with their miniguns.

INITIAL COMBAT ASSAULT BY ALLIED FORCES INTO THE A SHAU VALLEY, MAY 10, 1969 (PP.40–41)

Operation *Apache Snow* begins on the morning of May 10, 1969. Here a line of UH-1H Huey helicopters (**1**) inserts D/3/187th into a landing zone northwest of Dong Ap Bia. US infantry soldiers carrying packs, M-16 rifles, and a few M-60 machine guns dismount the helicopters and begin to secure the landing zone while AH-1G Cobra armed (**2**) and OH-6 light observations (**3**) helicopters fly overhead. The landings are unopposed and there are no North Vietnamese troops in sight. The company begins setting up its defenses while the accompanying battalion headquarters troops establish the battalion command post. D Company is followed by A and C Companies. (B Company remains in reserve at the brigade command post at Firebase Blaze.) Once on the ground, the soldiers move out to conduct reconnaissance in force operations to find the enemy.

Soldiers from 3rd Brigade, 101st Airborne, advance toward the base of Dong Ap Bia. (Bettmann/Getty Images)

At about the time the Cobras were firing on the NVA position, an NVA 12.7mm anti-aircraft machine gun opened fire on a forward air controller (FAC) aircraft orbiting to the east of Dong Ap Bia. The FAC called in two fighter-bombers which dropped four 500lb bombs, one of which landed on the NVA gun and its crew, destroying the position.

Lieutenant Colonel Honeycutt was unsure what his battalion was facing, but the picture was becoming clearer. The report of the action by the Cobras and the subsequent airstrike, along with the reports from A and C Companies about numerous bunkers and other evidence of NVA presence in the area, indicated to Honeycutt that his battalion had landed in an active base area and that the NVA was in the area in significant numbers.

Given the developing situation, Honeycutt believed he needed additional reinforcement. His B Company was being held in 3rd Brigade reserve at Firebase Blaze, so Honeycutt called the brigade commander, Colonel Conmy, to explain the situation and requested the release of his company. The brigade commander agreed, and Honeycutt had B Company picked up by 16 helicopters and inserted into an LZ east of Dong Ap Bia.

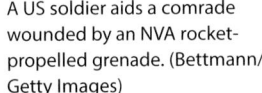

A US soldier aids a comrade wounded by an NVA rocket-propelled grenade. (Bettmann/Getty Images)

The helicopters carrying B Company arrived at the LZ at about 1600hrs. However, the movement was not without incident. On the way to the LZ, one of the Huey helicopters caught fire, and the pilot had to autorotate it down to the valley floor. Another helicopter landed to pick up the troops, but it was fired on as it climbed out of the valley and headed toward Ap Bia. The pilot was able to get the aircraft to the LZ.

An A-1E Skyraider dropping napalm and bombs to provide support to US and South Vietnamese troops during the attack on Dong Ap Bia (ullstein bild/Getty Images)

Having just landed, B Company began to deploy. It was immediately involved in a brief, but sharp firefight, which resulted in the death of two soldiers and the wounding of several others. The company's lead element moved off the LZ and started the 800m hike up the ridge toward the battalion CP. There, Honeycutt greeted the company commander, Captain Charles Littnan, and told him that he wanted B Company to take the top of Ap Bia so Honeycutt could move the battalion CP there the next morning.

At 1620hrs, B Company began the arduous climb up the narrow, steep trail toward the top of Ap Bia with 2nd Platoon in the lead. They soon ran into heavy fire from small arms and RPGs coming from farther up the trail. B Company returned fire and killed two NVA soldiers. Captain Littnan called in an airstrike, and two A-1 Skyraiders soon arrived on the scene. They bombed and strafed the ridge above B Company. By the time the A-1s finished, it was 1900hrs, and with darkness approaching, Honeycutt directed Littnan to set up a night defensive position (NDP) and prepare to continue the attack in the morning.

The company dug in on the high ground next to the LZ. As the unit set up its defensive positions for the night, one officer looked up the hill and remarked, "I think we are heading towards some pretty big shit." Subsequent events would prove him right.

By this time, there were six maneuver battalions (three US and three ARVN) operating in the A Shau Valley. Another ARVN battalion was scheduled for insertion on the following morning. Each of these units was assigned its area of operations with the mission of searching out and destroying the enemy and its defenses.

Back at the base of Dong Ap Bia, Honeycutt did not know that between 1,200 and 1,600 men of the 29th NVA Regiment and elements of several other units awaited the Rakkasans on the mountain. He assumed the North Vietnamese soldiers that B Company had encountered the previous day were only "trail watchers" or local small patrols. Regardless, he still wanted his CP on the mountaintop by early afternoon the next day.

DAY 2

The next morning, May 11, 3/187th resumed the attack with A and C Companies continuing their RIF operations. Initially, neither company made any contact with the NVA.

Per Honeycutt's orders from the night before, Captain Littnan and B Company began to move up the northern slope of Dong Ap Bia with

First Lieutenant Frank Boccia's 1st Platoon in the lead. Boccia's point man, Private First Class Terry Gann, probed cautiously up the narrow trail. As the platoon moved forward, it encountered dead North Vietnamese soldiers, blood trails, several weapons, and discarded equipment. Boccia went forward to check out the bodies. The dead NVA soldiers were young men in brand-new uniforms, with close-cropped hair indicating they had not been in the jungle long. Lying around them were two rifles, an RPG launcher, and six rocket grenades.

While exploring the surrounding area, the American soldiers discovered a packet of enemy documents. These were sent back to the battalion CP for evaluation by the intelligence officer. The intelligence officer, Captain Charles Addison, with help from Vinh, the battalion Kit Carson Scout (a former NVA soldier who had deserted and rallied to the allied side), quickly examined the documents, which identified the enemy force in the area as the 29th NVA Regiment. Vinh was frightened by this discovery because this regiment was known as "big American killers," and said there were "hundreds of soldiers" in the area. Honeycutt was undeterred by the news and defiantly told Vinh that he had come to kill North Vietnamese soldiers, and if there were a lot of them around, "they'll just be doing us a favor."

Not privy to this conversation at the time, Boccia changed out his point man with Specialist Fourth Class Phil Nelson, whom he considered the best tracker in the platoon, and continued up the steep slope of the ridge. As the platoon resumed its climb, it discovered several blood trails leading back up the mountain. It also ran into several piles of bloody bandages. These finds worried Boccia and his men. They had fought the NVA before but had never seen them leave such a clear trail as they withdrew from a firefight. Trooper Dennis Helms, Boccia's radio man, later recalled, "We had to go slow … We knew they were leading us into an ambush."

An AH-1G Cobra gunship flying over southern Vietnam in 1969; several Cobra gunships were involved in friendly fire incidents during the battle for Dong Ap Bia. (Pictures From History/Universal Images Group/Getty Images)

For Captain Littnan, it was taking too much time to check out the trail, so he told 1st Platoon to move faster. Boccia described the situation, saying they could not move any faster because they needed to figure out what was ahead on the trail. Somewhat mollified, Littnan told Boccia to do what he needed to do.

As 1st Platoon moved farther up the ridge, having taken an hour to cover 100m, it came to a clearing. Right in the center of it, there was a rucksack filled with rice balls, a brand-new AK-47 in a leather carrying case, a pile of banana clips for the rifle, and two Chicom grenades. This discovery, along with the earlier finds, extremely troubled Boccia. The NVA almost never left behind equipment. To Boccia, this was definitely beginning to look like a trap.

The company continued up the slopes, but Captain Littnan halted the advance shortly after noon for a short break so the troops could eat their rations and sit out a brief torrential rainstorm that had just started. After the rain stopped, the company began moving again, with 1st Platoon leading and Private First Class Nate Hyde on point. The rain made the trail very slippery and slowed down the already cautious movement of the unit.

As they moved up the mountain, the vegetation began to change. The bamboo that had hugged both sides of the trail gave way to giant teak trees, many well over 30m high. As the path opened up, visibility up the slope improved. Still, the platoon, not knowing exactly what was in front of it, continued to move carefully up the ridge.

The pace was unacceptable to Captain Littnan, who ordered 4th Platoon under Lieutenant Charles Denholm to leapfrog ahead of the 1st Platoon to take the lead up the mountain. The move was initially slowed by a lone NVA sniper who took the Americans under fire, but the unit returned fire and continued up the ridge. In the process, one of Denholm's men discovered a communications wire strung overhead in the bamboo and leading up the ridge to the top of the mountain, indicating the presence of a major NVA headquarters nearby.

Back at the LZ, Honeycutt met with Captain Addison, the brigade intelligence officer, who had arrived with a complete translation of the documents captured earlier. The translation clearly confirmed that the unit operating in the area was the 29th NVA Regiment, just as Vinh, the Kit Carson Scout, had said earlier. The documents further revealed that the regiment had recently returned from North Vietnam in April and had been conducting reconnaissance operations between Base Area 611 in Laos and the eastern end of the A Shau. Addison estimated the NVA strength in the area was between 1,200 and 1,800 men, but the documents did not mention exactly where the NVA was located. They did make it clear that the NVA was "definitely looking for a big fight." "Good," replied Honeycutt, "That's what we are lookin' for, too – a big fight!"

As B Company, with Denholm's platoon in the lead, continued up the narrow trail, a platoon from A Company, about 1,400m northwest of the battalion CP, found a major hard-packed road capable of handling truck traffic running west toward Laos and then east around the north side of the mountain. Tall jungle trees concealed the road with their tops woven and tied together to create a canopy overhead. Nearby, they discovered a hut and several bunkers that contained live chickens, clothing, and ammunition. A still-burning fire indicated that the NVA had only recently departed. All signs pointed to large numbers of NVA troops in the area.

At about 1600hrs, Denholm's platoon came under intense machine-gun and RPG fire from NVA troops dug into heavily fortified bunker positions up the hill; additional NVA soldiers popped up from spider holes and opened fire. Three American soldiers were killed in this engagement, and seven were wounded, including Lieutenant Denholm. Denholm and his men fell back down the trail a short way, leaving some of the wounded behind. Platoon Sergeant Louis Garza took charge of the situation and began to maneuver his men back up the trail to recover the casualties. They had to brave a steady hail of NVA fire as they tried to move forward, but by 1645hrs, they had retrieved the wounded soldiers.

Medics rush a wounded paratrooper to an LZ where he can be evacuated by helicopter. (Bettmann/Getty Images)

Captain Littnan called for artillery on the enemy positions. His forward observer (FO) crawled forward and adjusted the artillery, which pounded the area for 15 minutes. Then the FO marked his position with a smoke grenade and called in two Cobra aerial rocket artillery gunships to hit the area with their rockets.

For some unknown reason, the Cobras mistook the battalion's partially completed command post for the enemy and opened fire. Six rockets burst in the treetops, raining shrapnel down over a 30m area. Two Americans were killed, and 35 were wounded, including the S2, S3, and Honeycutt himself, who took a piece of shrapnel in his back. This would be the first of five friendly fire incidents caused by the thick jungle that made target identification very difficult.

Although wounded and in intense pain, Honeycutt refused evacuation and continued to command his battalion assisted by Major John Collier, the S3, who was wounded but also remained at the CP after the rest of the injured were evacuated. Honeycutt was understandably livid over the friendly fire incident. He called the brigade operations officer, Major Kenneth H. Montgomery, and, in a rage, threatened to shoot down any aircraft that approached the area without his express permission. In the middle of this tirade, four or five 120mm mortar shells struck the CP, indicating that the North Vietnamese had an FO with eyes on the battalion command group. Shortly after this, five NVA soldiers charged the CP area from the surrounding jungle. Troops from the battalion S2 section responded, killing three attackers and chasing the other NVA soldiers back into the jungle.

Given the day's events, Honeycutt had to reevaluate the situation. He wanted to continue the attack up the hill after pounding the NVA ahead of B Company with artillery, but he had lost his artillery FO in the friendly fire incident. With B Company just 200m from the enemy, but unable to move forward, Honeycutt ordered Littnan to pull back 100m to set up

Medics load wounded troopers into UH-1H Huey "Dust Off" for evacuation. (Bettmann/Getty Images)

defensive positions for the night and prepare to continue the attack the next morning.

Honeycutt had initially thought that Dong Ap Bia was being occupied by only a small force. However, the discoveries of bunkers and communications wire, coupled with the heavy contact with the NVA that B Company had endured, convinced Honeycutt that there was at least a reinforced platoon and maybe an entire company on the mountain. As the battle developed, it became clear that his revised estimate was still low.

Honeycutt wanted to find out what was exactly on the mountain, but not with just one company. He would send three companies up the mountain from three different directions. He directed A Company, commanded by Captain Gerald Harkins, to conduct a relief in place with D Company at the battalion CP; A Company would then serve as the battalion reserve. Once this change was accomplished, D Company would conduct a reconnaissance in force to the northeast and then due south up the north face of Hill 937. Meanwhile, C Company, commanded by Captain Dean Johnson, would conduct a RIF to the south and parallel with B Company, which would resume its advance toward the top of the hill. Thus, Honeycutt hoped to converge on Dong Ap Bia with a three-pronged attack.

Ideally, Honeycutt would have three companies in position by the morning of the 13th for a concerted push up the mountain. In

An NVA rocket explodes directly behind a trooper of the 101st Airborne, wounding him seriously during an assault on Dong Ap Bia. (Bettmann/Getty Images)

preparation for the next day's action, the Americans continued to bombard the hill with airstrikes and artillery, including napalm and delayed-fuze bombs.

Elsewhere in the valley, 1/506th, maneuvering near the Laotian border about 5km south of Hill 937, came under fire from 60mm and 82mm mortars. An on-call "Spooky" gunship took out the mortars, but not before 17 soldiers were wounded and had to be evacuated. The 2/501st Infantry had no contact with the NVA in its operations about 7km northwest of Hill 937.

During the night back at Dong Ap Bia, soldiers from B Company 3/187th saw and heard NVA soldiers on the slopes above them. Otherwise, it was pretty quiet. Honeycutt took advantage of the momentary lull in the action to order a medevac for himself. He was picked up and flown to Firebase Currahee, where the medics dug a thumb-sized chunk of shrapnel out of his back, relieving the pressure on the nerves that had made it difficult for him to walk. A helicopter then flew him back to the LZ on the northern side of the mountain just before daybreak.

On Dong Ap Bia, the NVA waited in concentric rows of bunkers, which afforded maximum utilization of the terrain and provided interlocking fields of fire down the mountain against the attackers. Additionally, it had placed command-detonated Soviet-made claymore mines along the major trails and positioned recoilless rifles at key positions in its defense. More importantly, it outnumbered the attackers.

DAY 3

Shortly after the sun rose over the A Shau on May 12, a flight of four A-1 Skyraiders flew in from the east to drop strings of 500lb bombs and canisters of napalm on the NVA in front of B Company. They strafed the jungle with

This time-lapse photo shows tracer-round trajectories from an Air Force Douglas AC-47D "Spooky" gunship. (Pictures from History/Universal Images Group/Getty Images)

their 20mm cannons as they departed the area. To the southwest, additional fighter-bombers hit the NVA in front of C Company.

After the airstrike, Captain Littnan, B Company commander, ordered his 1st Platoon to advance to the site of the strike, but to pull back if it met stiff resistance. Led by Lieutenant Boccia, the platoon headed up the mountain, now pockmarked by bomb holes and still burning in places. Nearing the site of the previous day's fight, they encountered a North Vietnamese log bunker. One of the troopers set up a 90mm recoilless rifle and fired two rounds at the bunker, partially destroying it.

This was like kicking over an anthill. Scores of North Vietnamese soldiers swarmed from their spider holes and trenches, opening fire on the Americans with RPGs and heavy machine guns; in a matter of seconds, six men were wounded. One of the RPGs scored a direct hit on the recoilless rifle, but miraculously, the two soldiers manning the gun survived without injuries.

The battalion called in artillery and attack helicopters to dislodge the NVA from its fortified positions. Still, the NVA soldiers continued to place effective automatic weapons and a barrage of RPG fire on the Americans. To make matters worse, the NVA lobbed mortar shells into the attackers. Lieutenant Boccia later recalled, "We tried to shoot back, but the assault was too intense. I couldn't even lift my head."

Boccia ordered his men to fall back in the face of the heavy fire. As they pulled back toward the previous night's defensive position, dragging their wounded with them, a flight of fighter-bombers pounded the entrenched North Vietnamese soldiers with an array of ordnance, including high-drag bombs and napalm. As Boccia and his men withdrew, Honeycutt called for another strike against the top of Hill 937.

At about 1230hrs, fighter-bombers hit the NVA with 1,000lb bombs with delay fuzes. Then ten artillery battalions pounded the hill for 30 minutes. When the artillery shelling ceased, two pairs of Cobra gunships hit the mountain with rockets and miniguns. At 1400hrs, another wave of fighter-bombers returned and hit the entrenchments.

Airmen loading ammunition into one of the three 7.62mm cannons that are mounted on the side of an Air Force Douglas AC-47 "Spooky" gunship. (Underwood Archives/Getty Images)

After the Cobras cleared the area, 2nd Platoon from B Company, led by Lieutenant Marshall Eward, started up the hill. Although Eward figured the pounding by artillery, fighter-bombers, and the Cobras had sufficiently softened up the NVA, his platoon was soon taken under heavy fire and forced back.

Honeycutt ordered a group of engineers to cut an LZ in the jungle closer to B Company's position. This would better facilitate resupply and help with the more timely evacuation of the wounded as the company moved up the mountain. As the helicopter carrying the engineers hovered over the chosen site, they started to rappel down from the aircraft laden with their tools. The first man made it down safely, but when the second man started down the rope, the North Vietnamese opened up with machine guns. The helicopter pilot banked frantically away, and the dangling engineer fell through the jungle canopy, shattering both legs when he hit the ground.

In response, Honeycutt ordered his forward air controller to "Dump the world on their asses!" The FAC called in a flight of four fighter-bombers, which dropped 30 500lb bombs on the NVA positions. After the strike, the helicopter carrying the engineers made another approach to the LZ site, but an RPG lashed out from the mountainside, shattering the chopper's rotor and sending it to the ground. All six engineers and the four crew members were seriously injured in the crash, but B Company's men rescued them before the helicopter caught fire and exploded.

Honeycutt requested another strike on the NVA positions on the mountain above B Company. A new flight of fighter-bombers dropped 1,000lb bombs on the North Vietnamese. As they cleared the area, ten howitzer batteries again opened up on the mountain in a hail of fire that lasted for a half-hour. Then Cobra gunships arrived and raked the North Vietnamese positions with thousands of rounds from their miniguns. As the attack helicopters pulled off, another group of fighter-bombers arrived and pounded the mountain with more 1,000lb bombs.

Meanwhile, the NVA had halted C and D Companies short of their attack positions for the planned May 13 assault up the mountain. C Company was harassed every step of the way by NVA snipers and sustained eight wounded in an RPG ambush. The company commander called for mortars on the enemy positions, then gunships and artillery. One of the artillery rounds must have struck an NVA ammo cache, because a secondary explosion went off in the NVA line. As some of the NVA fled, C Company pushed forward, but it advanced only about 75m when a flurry of RPGs again hit it. The North Vietnamese soldiers fired the RPGs into the treetops, which sprayed the Americans with shrapnel, wounding eight men. C Company was effectively stopped and dug in for the night approximately 200m south of B Company.

Having been relieved from securing the battalion CP, D Company was having a worse time. The ever-present NVA snipers harassed them as they tried to negotiate the almost impassable terrain. The company took over five hours to advance 500m and its pace was slowing, rather than quickening. It was still in no position to support the main attack on Hill 937.

The thick foliage and close proximity of friendly troops inhibited the use and effectiveness of indirect fire, making it very difficult to make anything but slow progress. At this point, it was clear that the Americans had grossly underestimated the strength of the NVA on the hill; it was much stronger than anticipated, much more than company strength, and seemed to be getting stronger every day as additional reinforcements arrived from Laos.

While 3/187th was trying to force its way up Hill 937, the NVA also struck at Firebase Airborne on Dong Ngai, a mountain just a few kilometers north of Dong Ap Bia. One of the five firebases established to support *Apache Snow*, Airborne, which had been blasted out of hilltop jungle by a "Daisy Cutter" bomb, was defended by A Company, 2/501st Infantry, commanded by Captain Gordon C. Johnson, and was manned by three field artillery batteries, including four 155mm

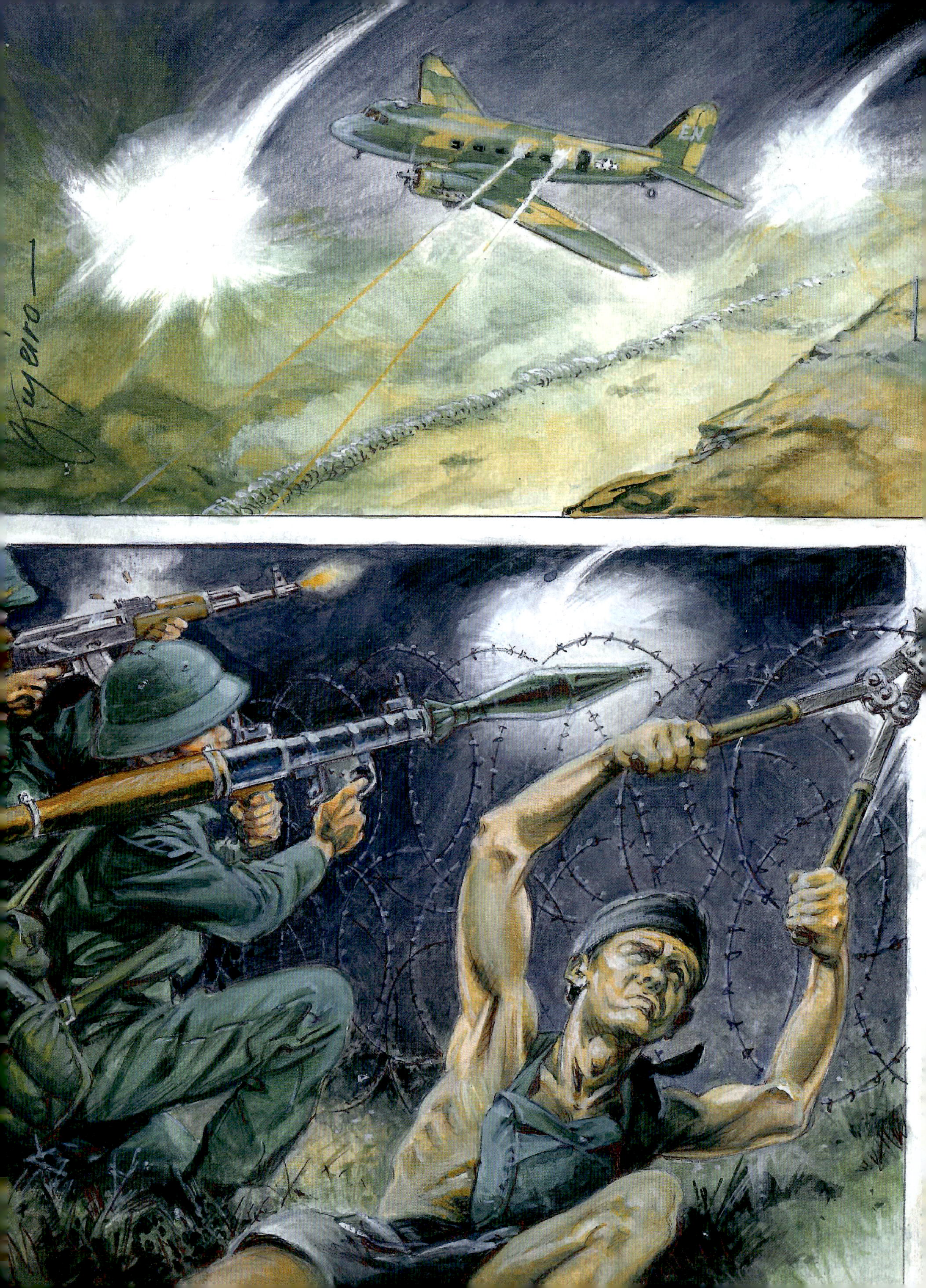

SAPPER ATTACK ON FIREBASE AIRBORNE, MAY 13, 1969 (PP.52–53)

In the early morning hours of May 13, North Vietnamese troops from the K-12 Sapper Battalion and elements of the 806th NVA Battalion attack Firebase Airborne, located on Dong Ngai, a mountain just a few kilometers north of Dong Ap Bia. The firebase had been blasted out of a hilltop jungle by a "Daisy Cutter" bomb. It was defended by A/2/501st Infantry and manned by three field artillery batteries, including four 155mm howitzers from C/2/11th Field Artillery, six 105mm howitzers from C/2/319th Field Artillery, and two 105mm howitzers from B/2/319th Field Artillery. The enemy sappers breach the protective wire (**1**). Other NVA soldiers armed with AK-47s, RPK machineguns, and B-40 rocket launchers (RPGs) are behind the sappers (**2**). The North Vietnamese pour into the firebase and begin hurling grenades and satchel charges into the American bunkers and gun emplacements. Under star shells fired by the 81mm mortar platoon, the Americans fight a desperate battle with the attackers. The defenders eventually turn back the attack with support from an AC-47 "Spooky" gunship (**3**).

howitzers from Battery C, 2/11th Field Artillery, six 105mm howitzers from Battery C, 2/319th Field Artillery, and two 105mm howitzers from Battery B, 2/319th Field Artillery.

In the early morning of May 13, sappers from the K-12 Sapper Battalion crawled forward and cut a half-dozen approaches in the firebase's protective concertina wire without the American guards detecting them. Following a barrage from the supporting NVA 82mm mortars, elements of the 806th NVA Battalion from the 6th NVA Regiment, which had remained in the area after the majority of the regiment had departed for Laos, swarmed into the firebase, firing RPGs and hurling grenades and satchel charges into American bunkers. Two sergeants, Roger Barski and Kenneth Counts, squad leaders in 1st Platoon, A Company, managed to organize a defense, and then, joining with a small group of men under Lieutenant Howard Pitts, 2nd Platoon Leader, they counterattacked.

Illuminated by star shells fired by the 81mm mortar platoon, the Americans fought back as the battle seesawed back and forth. The tide turned when an AC-47 "Spooky" gunship arrived on the scene and began pouring devastating fire into the North Vietnamese infantry attempting to move up to join the sappers in overrunning the firebase. In the face of devastating fire from the gunship's 7.62mm miniguns, the NVA sappers and infantry withdrew, leaving 39 dead inside the perimeter and a dozen more draped over the wire. The US lost 22 killed and 61 wounded; among the dead were the battery commander and first sergeant from Battery C, 2/319th Field Artillery, killed when the battery fire direction center took a direct hit from an RPG. The survivors were then gunned down by an NVA soldier. Five howitzers were damaged in the fighting.

Based on body count, the fight had been a victory for the Americans, but as Colonel Conmy recalled in an interview after the war, "We held the firebase, but it was the worst result from a sapper attack that I have ever seen." In the aftermath of the attack, Conmy airlifted the rest of the 2/501st from its area of operations along the Laotian border and inserted it near the firebase to protect the base and search for and destroy any remaining NVA forces in the area.

At division headquarters, Major General Zais, overseeing the progress of *Apache Snow*, viewed the attack on Firebase Airborne as another sign that the area around Dong Ap Bia was a critical base for the NVA and that it would fight hard to protect it. Despite being bombed, napalmed, strafed, and bombarded with artillery for three days, the North Vietnamese were no closer to being subdued. It was clear they were not going to give up without a fight to the death. It was also clear to him that Ap Bia was occupied by more NVA than the 3/187th could handle alone. Accordingly, he ordered the 1/506th north from its area of operations to assist Honeycutt by attacking cross-country to hit the NVA facing 3/187th from the rear and preclude the NVA from reinforcing Dong Ap Bia.

Conmy expected that the 1/506th, starting from its location some 4,800m south of Hill 937 near the A Sap River, would be able to provide some relief to 3/187th no later than the morning of May 15. However, as it turned out, it would take five and a half days, until May 19, for 1/506th to reach a position where it could support the Rakkasans due to constant NVA contact and rough terrain.

DAY 4

Meanwhile, Honeycutt believed that he had to do something other than wait for the arrival of his sister battalion; he did not want to give the NVA a chance to reinforce and strengthen its positions on the mountain. At daybreak on May 13, 3/187th launched another attack on Dong Ap Bia with three companies. Honeycutt ordered B Company to continue its attack up the main ridge while C Company was to launch another attack up a small finger 150m south of B Company. He directed D Company to move back down the ravine where it was located and attempt to launch a flanking attack up the north side of the mountain.

At 0656hrs, a forward air controller appeared overhead and, guided by a smoke grenade thrown by Lieutenant Eward, marked the target with a phosphorus rocket. Then two F-4 Phantom jets dropped 1,000lb bombs with delayed-action fuzes. Captain Littnan directed Lieutenant Boccia and his platoon to move forward immediately following the end of the airstrike.

On its flank to the west, C Company initially made rapid progress toward its objective, but the NVA quickly counterattacked, and in the ensuing fight, the US unit suffered several dead and wounded. Using the same tactics it had used against B Company, the NVA fired RPGs into the trees, showering the Americans with deadly shrapnel. During the battle, NVA gunners in bunkers hidden in the ravine between C and B Companies poured effective enfilading fire into C Company.

Honeycutt ordered B Company to drop down on the east side of its ridge to put the ridge between it and the NVA. He then called for an airstrike against the bunkers firing on C Company. The incoming aircraft dropped bombs on the bunkers, smashing them; however, one of the bombs fell too close to B Company, killing one man and wounding several others in the 1st Platoon.

With 1st Platoon momentarily incapacitated by the errant bomb strike, Captain Littnan moved Lieutenant Eward's 2nd Platoon forward.

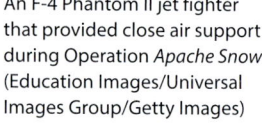

An F-4 Phantom II jet fighter that provided close air support during Operation *Apache Snow*. (Education Images/Universal Images Group/Getty Images)

Third assault on Hill 937, May 13, 1969

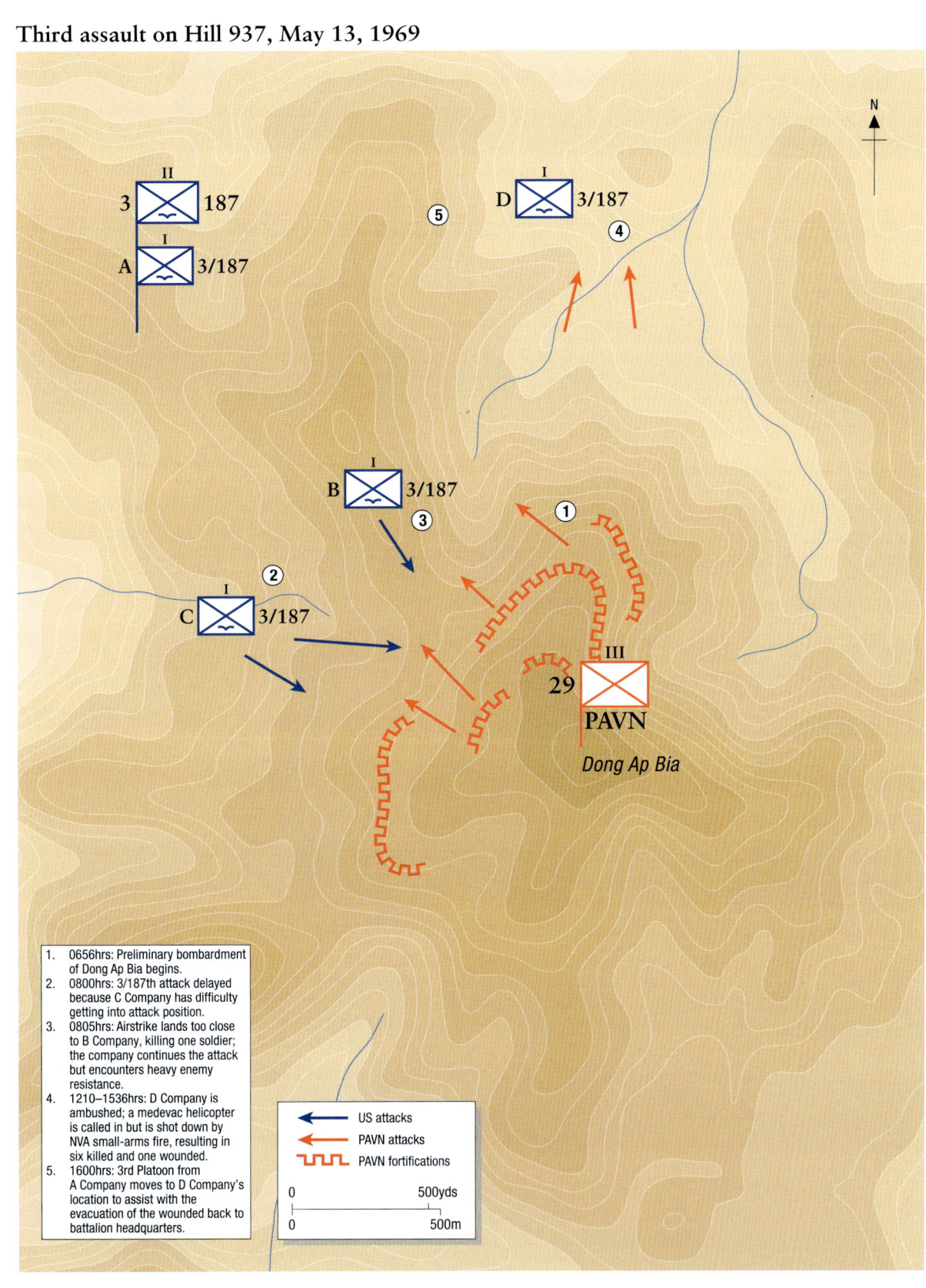

A medical evacuation helicopter sets down in a tiny clearing in the A Shau Valley to pick up wounded soldiers from the 101st Airborne Division. (Bettmann/Getty Images)

With friendly artillery continuing to pound NVA positions and Cobra helicopters in support, B Company attempted to move up the hill again. It came under effective sniper fire almost immediately. Eward rushed two of his squads forward, forming a skirmish line, firing as they inched forward. They had gone about 20m when the North Vietnamese came out of their holes and cut loose with RPGs, grenades, and withering rifle and machine-gun fire. Three men were hit instantly, and the platoon pulled back.

At the same time, C Company also attempted to maneuver toward the objective. However, like B Company, C Company was stopped by intense fire and eventually fell back as the NVA fired AK-47s and RPGs while rolling grenades down the steep slopes at the Americans.

The rugged terrain and constant NVA machine-gun and RPG fire also severely hampered D Company, struggling to get into its assigned attack position. Battling against steep terrain and thick undergrowth, the lead platoon reached the bottom of the ravine and crossed a creek about 900m

Four US soldiers keep low as they rush a stretcher-borne wounded comrade to a medical aid station during the battle for Dong Ap Bia. (Bettmann/Getty Images)

north of B Company. While taking a brief halt for lunch, the platoon came under mortar fire and still more RPGs. Seven men were wounded. The platoon paused to airlift out their casualties, but the NVA hit the medevac helicopter from the 326th Medical Battalion with an RPG while it was hovering to pick up the wounded. The helicopter fell on the men below, crushing several to death, then exploded, killing several men on board, including two wounded troopers from D Company who had been previously picked up by the medevac.

D Company soldiers pulled the pilot, Lieutenant Gerald Torba, free of the helicopter wreckage before it exploded, but he was severely burned, and his left leg was crushed. They carried Torba with them for a time, but they eventually believed he had died from his burns and placed him on a pile of dead NVA for later retrieval. Torba ultimately survived after he was found alive 17 hours later by other Americans and evacuated. He would eventually lose his leg but stay in the military.

Shortly after the helicopter was downed, the NVA, realizing D Company's vulnerability in the ravine, swarmed from its bunkers and spider holes, pouring down rifle, machine-gun, and RPG fire on the Americans. Captain Luther Sanders, the company commander, called in an airstrike, and the incoming fighter-bombers caught the attacking North Vietnamese in the open and strafed them with cannon fire. The area was strewn with dead and dying North Vietnamese as the surviving soldiers fled back up the mountain.

D Company gathered its casualties and, carrying the seriously wounded, withdrew back the way it had come up the ravine on the other side of the creek toward the battalion CP. It was joined by A Company's 3rd Platoon, who had been dispatched to provide assistance. By 2000hrs, they had reached the edge of their defensive position from the night before. Then it started to rain. In the ensuing downpour, they were unable to move up the 45-degree slope in the mud. They had to halt and set up an NDP; evacuation of the wounded had to wait until the following day.

In C Company, 1st Platoon, under Lieutenant Joel Trautman, began cutting an LZ on the ridge immediately behind the company's forward line for easier resupply and medevac. A platoon of NVA soldiers slipped around the company's flank and opened fire on the Americans at the LZ site, killing two and wounding five more. Lieutenant Trautman led a counterattack that drove them off.

At this point, the day's attack by 3/187th had stalled. The 350 men of the battalion could not overcome the fire superiority of the 1,200 or more North Vietnamese heavily entrenched on the slopes of Dong Ap Bia above them. During the day's fighting, 12 Rakkasans were killed, and more than 80 were wounded.

Both Honeycutt and Conmy realized that the North Vietnamese, who usually fought hard for a while before quitting the battlefield, were

Wounded troopers make their way down Dong Ap Bia with the help of medics. (Bettmann/Getty Images)

planning to stand and fight on Dong Ap Bia. The NVA gave no sign of quitting the fight.

Honeycutt's troopers had suffered heavy casualties, but had not gained much ground in the bitter fighting. Sure that "the NVA were present in considerable strength in the vicinity of Hill 937," Honeycutt knew that his troops were heavily outnumbered, and he told Conmy, "I don't have the manpower to stop them." He implored the brigade commander to tell the 1/506th "to get their asses in gear."

When the sun went down on the 13th, the Rakkasans could see the NVA cooking fires that dotted the mountainside above them; one trooper estimated that there were over 100 of them that ran in three irregular rows around the mountain. The North Vietnamese were still there and did not care if the paratroopers knew it; they would be waiting for the Rakkasans when they tried to take the hill again. During the night, an AC-47 "Spooky" gunship was called in to take the enemy under fire with its miniguns. After it cleared the area, artillery continued to pound them as well.

At the battalion CP, Honeycutt was monitoring reports from his companies when a Vietnamese voice broke in on the net. Using a captured US radio, the North Vietnamese hailed Honeycutt, referring to him by his call sign, "Blackjack," and mocking him and his men.

Honeycutt was too busy to pay much attention to the North Vietnamese heckler on the radio. He believed that the NVA was continually strengthening its defenses and that it would be harder, not easier, to dislodge it as time passed. Therefore, he planned to renew the attack the next morning rather than wait.

The battalion plan called for a simultaneous assault up the mountain by B Company from the west, C Company also from the west but up a small ridge 150m south of B Company, and D Company, once it evacuated its wounded and dead, was to move back down the ravine, back across the creek bottom, and attempt once again to attack up the mountain from the north.

A chaplain conducts a religious service under the shadow of an artillery piece at a firebase supporting operations in the A Shau Valley. (Bettmann/Getty Images)

Honeycutt hoped that the NVA would be unable to concentrate its forces against such a widespread attack. He had requested that the 1/506th attempt to block movement through the large draw on the southwest side of Hill 900 that the NVA had been using to move fresh troops and supplies up the mountain at night. However, 1/506th had yet to advance close enough to the mountain to do so; it was still over 2km south of Hill 937. For now, 3/187th was on its own.

DAY 5

Preceding the attack was a massive artillery preparation on each of the planned routes of advance. At first light on the 14th, every battery on the five supporting firebases opened up, firing volley after volley into the top and west face of the mountain.

When the artillery ceased at 0646hrs, fighter-bombers hit the upper slopes and top of the mountain with "Snake and Nape," 500lb and 1,000lb high-drag bombs and napalm. For the next hour, several flights of fighter-bombers worked over the mountain.

Shortly after 0800hrs, after the fighter-bombers had completed their runs, all three companies launched their attacks up the mountain. The attackers dropped their rucksacks, carrying only their weapons, ammunition, and water, and pushed up the 45-degree slope.

B Company attacked with Lieutenant Eward's 2nd Platoon in the lead. The attackers immediately bogged down when they encountered heavy North Vietnamese fire. The platoon tried to push forward, but the NVA detonated Soviet-made MON-100 claymore mines hanging in the trees still standing. The lethal blasts from these crudely made weapons sent deadly shrapnel into the platoon, wounding several men. Eward and his men regrouped and again attempted to advance when the NVA detonated more mines, wounding three more men. On 2nd Platoon's flank, 4th Platoon, led by Sergeant First Class Louis Garza, who had taken over after Lieutenant Denholm was wounded, also tried to advance. However, neither platoon could make any progress against the intense NVA fire.

At the same time, the NVA also hit Lieutenant Boccia's 1st Platoon, which was guarding the LZ and attempting to bring ammunition forward. With all of his platoons under fire, Captain Littnan, the B Company commander, decided to pull his forward platoons back and attempt to regroup.

On B Company's western flank, C Company, commanded by Captain Dean Johnson, headed up a small ridge, led by Lieutenant Goff's 3rd Platoon, followed by Lieutenant Sullivan's 2nd Platoon. Goff's platoon ran into heavy fire from three NVA bunkers about 20m up the ridge. Pressing the attack, Goff's troops knocked out all three bunkers with 90mm recoilless rifles, firing flechette rounds.

Having taken out the first line of bunkers, 2nd Platoon advanced rapidly about 150m and then turned up the western flank of Hill 900, adjacent and slightly lower than Hill 937. This terrain formed a natural path for North Vietnamese reinforcement and resupply of Dong Ap Bia from Laos to the west. This path was guarded by two rows of mutually supporting bunkers. As Goff directed his men forward, they came under withering fire and a flurry of grenades and RPG fire.

Wounded US soldiers receive medical attention as they await evacuation during the bitter fighting for Dong Ap Bia. (Bettmann/Getty Images)

Nevertheless, C Company continued to press forward. Using its 90mm recoilless rifles, the company systematically took out the bunkers, but suffered six wounded in the process. Captain Johnson reported to battalion that he was 40m from the top of Hill 900. However, shortly after he made the call on the radio, the NVA counterattacked. One group of NVA poured down the hill directly into the 3rd Platoon, while a second group assaulted the platoon's rear. Another group began pouring enfilading fire into the platoon's left flank. Johnson reported that he had lost two killed in action and 15 wounded, and that he was in danger of being overrun from the rear and was withdrawing. Honeycutt denied Johnson the permission to withdraw and told him to get his other two platoons into the fight.

With C Company in trouble, B Company was forced to halt its advance to come to its aid. Honeycutt told Captain Littnan to send his 1st Platoon to assist C Company. The remainder of B Company, led by 4th Platoon, continued to push up the mountain against intense NVA fire.

Boccia and his platoon, moving up the mountain, turned to cross the mountain face toward C Company down the south side of the ridge. Boccia soon realized that they were blocked by an NVA unit about 25m in front of them that was firing into C Company's rear on the ridge just above them. He decided to move his unit to the west to find another route to C Company. As they moved up the other side of the ridge, Boccia called in mortars and artillery on the NVA positions firing on C Company's rear.

A US soldier fires an M-79 grenade launcher at a suspected enemy position near an LZ in the A Shau. (Bettmann/Getty Images)

As Boccia and his platoon tried to work their way toward C Company, the situation there worsened. Captain Johnson had two platoons that were effectively pinned down by heavy fire. Very quickly, they sustained two killed and 30 wounded. Johnson again asked for permission to withdraw; given the company's state, Honeycutt had no choice except to permit it to pull back. As the company attempted to withdraw, the NVA attacked those trying to evacuate the wounded. The 1st Platoon Leader, Lieutenant Trautman, came forward and took charge of the withdrawal. At about 1400hrs, he began to pull the company back into a defensive position.

By 1600hrs, Lieutenant Boccia and his men linked up with C Company at its company CP. There, an LZ had been set up to evacuate the dead and wounded. Boccia was stunned that there were 20 to 30 dead and wounded on the ground, with no one providing security. Boccia later remembered thinking that "Charlie Company had disintegrated." He had two of his squads establish security around the LZ, while C Company prepared to evacuate its first sergeant, two platoon leaders, the company executive officer, two platoon sergeants, six squad leaders, and 40 enlisted men.

Honeycutt directed Boccia to get all the wounded out with as much of their gear as possible and to burn the rest. After that, he was to collect the C Company survivors and move back to B Company's NDP. Boccia did as he was ordered; his platoon and the remnants of C Company arrived at B Company's position at about 2130hrs.

While Boccia and his platoon were coming to the aid of C Company, the rest of B Company was having its own problems. Captain Littnan called in airstrikes and a 15-minute artillery prep. Then Sergeant Garza led the men of 4th Platoon forward for yet another assault. Garza, an experienced soldier well thought-of in the unit, led three consecutive attempts to move up the hill, but each time they ran into a hail of fire from a line of bunkers to their front, sustaining seven wounded in the process. Leading a smaller group, Garza tried again, moving forward and taking out several snipers hiding in the treetops before reaching the NVA bunker line. There they saw the devastation wrought by the artillery and airstrikes. Amid the wreckage were body parts and splashes of blood. The bombardment had been very effective.

However, the NVA was far from finished. As the 4th Platoon consolidated its position, the North Vietnamese opened up from a second line of bunkers only 30m farther up the ridge. At this time, Lieutenant Colonel Honeycutt, concerned that C Company's withdrawal now exposed B Company's right flank, radioed Captain Littnan and told him likewise to withdraw.

Elsewhere, things were not much better. D Company's attack up the north face of Hill 937 was again halted at the river by intense machine-gun and RPG fire. Having sustained seven wounded, Captain Sanders called for artillery and air support to suppress the enemy fire. The fire lessened after several airstrikes, artillery barrages, and runs by Cobra gunships. However, the company had sustained ten more wounded and could not move forward.

A group of soldiers continues its sweep of one of the hills surrounding Dong Ap Bia in the A Shau Valley. (Bettmann/Getty Images)

Sanders requested and received permission to withdraw and bring his wounded back.

Two Cobra gunships that were supposed to be supporting 1/506th as it moved overland to reinforce 3/187th became disoriented. Spotting B Company retreating down Hill 937 and a platoon from A Company that had been dispatched to help B Company carry its wounded, the Cobras mistook the Americans for North Vietnamese moving to block 1/506th. They rolled in with their miniguns blazing, severely wounding four Americans before they could be called off.

Honeycutt again went into a rage, shouting on the radio, "Jesus Christ! What the fuck is going on around here? This is turning into a goddamn three-ring circus!" Then he angrily reiterated his threat to shoot down any unauthorized helicopter or other aircraft approaching his men. His men had been fighting for their lives against the NVA, and now they had to worry about being fired on by their own supporting aircraft.

By late afternoon, Honeycutt's three forward companies had withdrawn and began to set up defensive positions in preparation for the next day's attack. The American troops had fought bravely, but the Rakkasans simply lacked the manpower to overcome the superior numbers of North Vietnamese troops, who had enough men to block all three attacking companies simultaneously.

After repeated attempts without success to take the mountain, troop morale plummeted. Some soldiers began questioning their orders, convinced that the whole mission was senseless. To make matters worse, at about 1700hrs, a powerful rainstorm broke over the mountain. That night, the Americans observed numerous cooking fires on the slopes above them; these fires were just another indicator that they were facing a large number of NVA soldiers who planned to stay and fight.

Honeycutt called each of his company commanders for a final casualty count. During the day's hard fighting, his companies had sustained 12 men killed and over 80 wounded, but had still not gained any ground. The NVA had also taken some heavy losses, but to Honeycutt, it seemed to be getting stronger every day.

Just before dark, Colonel Conmy, the 3rd Brigade commander, arrived at the LZ by helicopter. Honeycutt met him and brought him to his CP, where he gave the brigade commander a situation update. Honeycutt told Conmy that his battalion did not have the manpower to stop the NVA from moving fresh troops in from Laos every night, saying, "The 506th has got to get their asses in gear and get involved in the fight." Conmy told Honeycutt that 1/506th was still en route and that two ARVN battalions would also enter the fight.

As Conmy was meeting with Honeycutt, Major General Zais, at division headquarters at Camp Eagle, conferred with Brigadier General Jim Smith, the assistant division commander, about the advisability of continuing the battle for Dong Ap Bia. Zais was under pressure from sources outside the division to pull out of the fight. Smith, who had already spent two and a half years in Vietnam and was very familiar with North Vietnamese tactics, advised Zais to see the battle through "to a successful conclusion." Zais took his advice, and this would later prove to be a very controversial decision.

Back at Dong Ap Bia, Honeycutt hoped to keep the pressure on the NVA. Realizing that C Company was battered and exhausted from the heavy fighting that it had endured, Honeycutt pulled the remnants of the company out of the defensive line under cover of darkness and had them take up positions around the battalion CP. He then ordered A Company to move forward to occupy C Company's former position on B Company's southern flank to prepare for a renewed attack up the southern ridgeline.

Honeycutt received several reports about NVA movements during the night. From these reports, he believed that the NVA would try to position a large force in the ravine between B and C Companies' old position and then attack both companies in the rear as they continued to attack up the mountain. Honeycutt planned an ambush to take the NVA by surprise.

Later that night, however, Honeycutt got some bad news when he was told that the 1/506th was still nearly 2km from Dong Ap Bia. It had been on the move since the 13th, and Honeycutt had hoped it would be able to cut the NVA supply lines from Laos and launch another attack on the mountain from the south. However, it had managed to advance only 1,500m and was still not in a position to assist 3/187th in the attack. There would also be no help from 2/501st, which had been withdrawn to the Firebase Airborne area after the attack there on the 13th. Honeycutt knew that 3/187th was still on its own. Keenly aware that time was not on his side, he decided to push forward with the attack, rather than wait for the 1/506th.

DAYS 6–7

At noon on May 15, after a heavy artillery bombardment and several airstrikes, A and B Companies began their advance up the hill as if for another assault. However, per Honeycutt's ambush plan, after going a short distance, they quietly halted and deployed facing each other, weapons pointed down into the ravine between their respective ridges. Honeycutt's trap was set.

As Honeycutt had anticipated, a large number of NVA soldiers swarmed out of the ravine on both sides. Instead of finding the Americans headed up the slopes and facing away from them, they walked into the fields of fire of A and B Companies facing them. The heavy fire from the Americans shocked the NVA, and it retreated back into the ravine. Honeycutt had another surprise for it; he had a pair of fighter-bombers orbiting nearby and called them in. They strafed the NVA with their 20mm cannons and then made a second run, dropping napalm and 500lb bombs. They finished up with another strafing run. Once the aircraft cleared the area, Honeycutt's artillery liaison officer called in a rolling artillery barrage from 105mm, 155mm, and 8in howitzers that ranged up and down the ravine. To complete the ambush, two Cobra gunships sprayed the area with their miniguns. In very short order, an entire NVA company was wiped out.

At 1320hrs with the fires still burning in the ravine, A and B Companies resumed their attack up the mountain, preceded by yet another artillery barrage on the top of the mountain. However, the NVA recovered quickly and poured heavy fire from newly dug spider holes and hastily reconstructed bunkers. Additionally, it triggered command-detonated claymore mines, which the NVA had emplaced during the night. These caused several casualties, particularly in B Company.

Still, the American attackers pushed up the mountain aided by several effective airstrikes. They moved steadily forward, firing into the trees to take

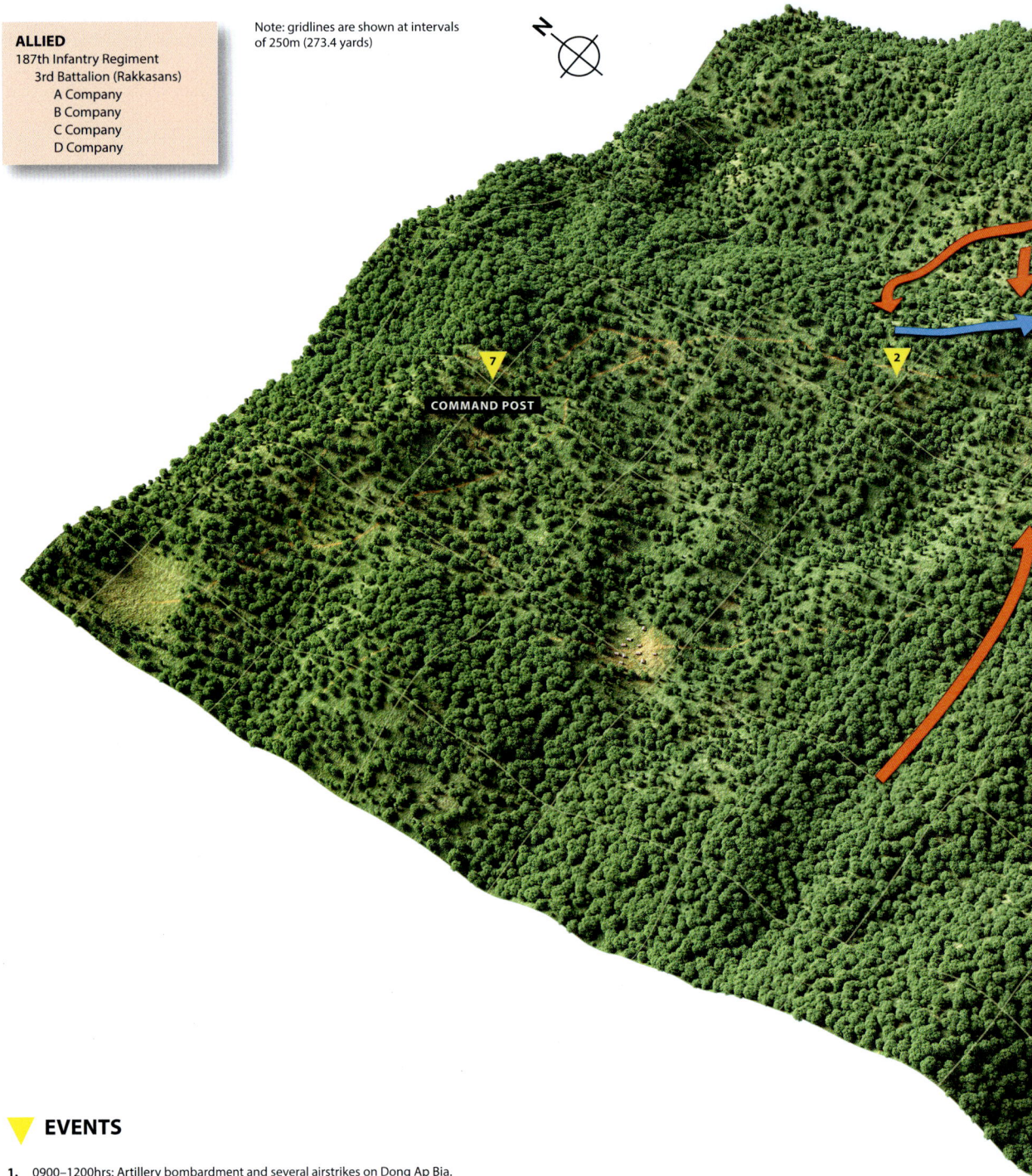

ALLIED
187th Infantry Regiment
    3rd Battalion (Rakkasans)
        A Company
        B Company
        C Company
        D Company

Note: gridlines are shown at intervals of 250m (273.4 yards)

EVENTS

1. 0900–1200hrs: Artillery bombardment and several airstrikes on Dong Ap Bia.
2. 1200hrs: A and B Companies begin their assaults up the hill.
3. 1210hrs: A and B Companies turn toward the ravine between them and prepare to fire on the North Vietnamese. The night before Lieutenant Colonel Honeycutt anticipated that the NVA would come up the ravine, and so the move by A and B Companies was part of a trap to catch the enemy by surprise. When the North Vietnamese swarm up the ravine, they are met by devastating fire from the American troops. Honeycutt follows up the ambush with airstrikes and artillery. During this action, an entire NVA company is wiped out.
4. 1320hrs: B Company resumes its assault up the hill but the North Vietnamese recover quickly, pouring heavy fire on the attackers and triggering command-detonated claymore mines, which the NVA had emplaced during the night.
5. 1400hrs: B Company request attack helicopter support; Cobra gunships arrive and mistakenly fire on B Company, wounding the company commander.
6. 1630hrs: A Company, which had been on B Company's right flank, fights a pitched battle with entrenched North Vietnamese troops but pulls back to evacuate the wounded.
7. Lieutenant Colonel Honeycutt suspends the attack and withdraws his forces into night defensive positions. Close air support and artillery continue to pound the hill during the night.

THE FIFTH ASSAULT UP DONG AP BIA, MAY 15, 1969

On May 15, the Rakkasans launched their fifth assault up Dong Ap Bia beginning at 0900hrs with a three-hour artillery prep of the mountain. At 1200hrs, A and B Companies began their attack.

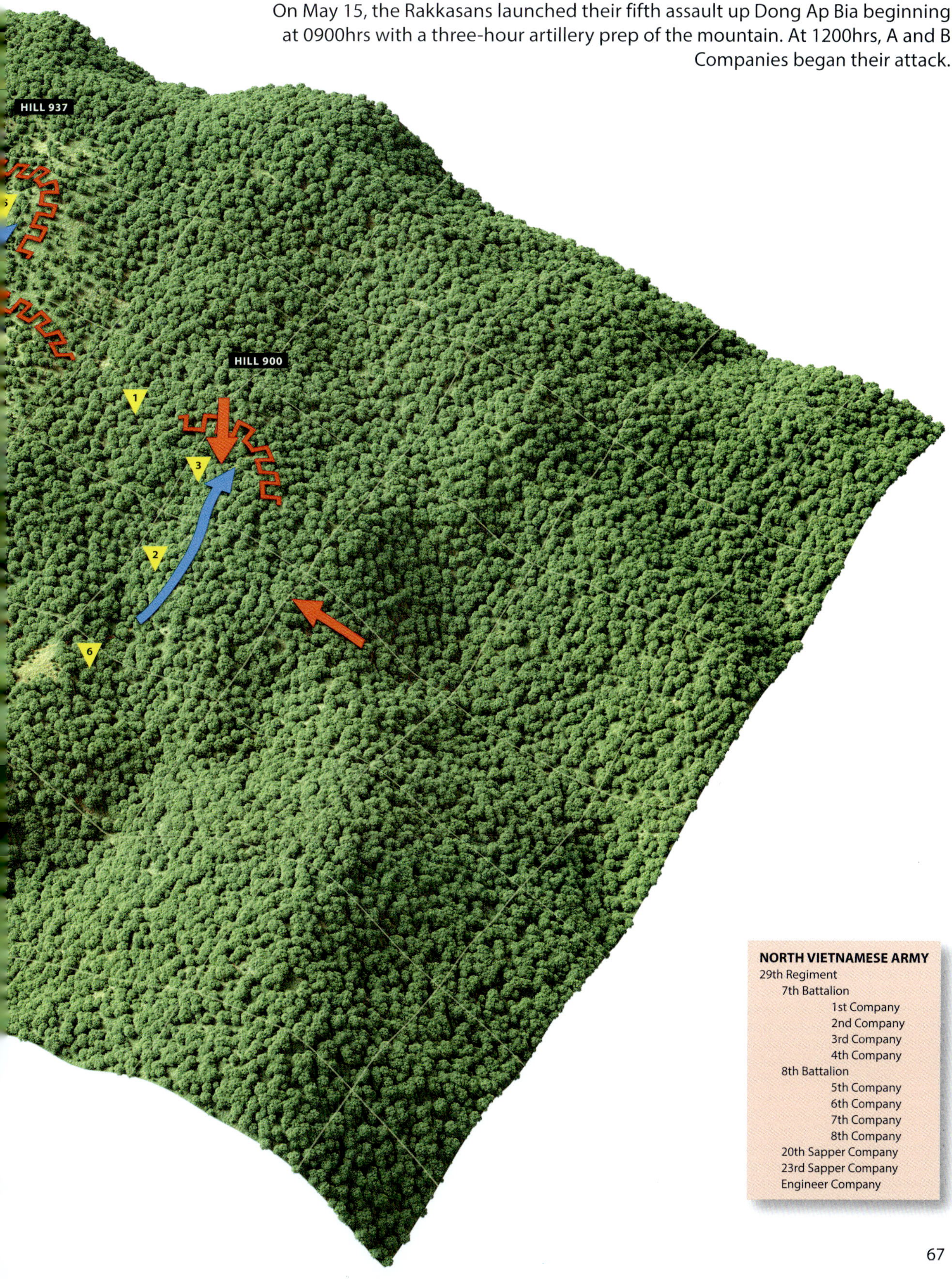

HILL 937

HILL 900

NORTH VIETNAMESE ARMY
29th Regiment
  7th Battalion
    1st Company
    2nd Company
    3rd Company
    4th Company
  8th Battalion
    5th Company
    6th Company
    7th Company
    8th Company
  20th Sapper Company
  23rd Sapper Company
  Engineer Company

out NVA snipers and using recoilless rifles against the bunkers. Led by Sergeant Garza, the 4th Platoon got to within 150m of the top of Dong Ap Bia. There it was pinned down by a second line of bunkers. Garza called Captain Littnan and requested gunships to take out the bunkers. Littnan called in the Cobras to hit the bunkers in front of the 4th Platoon. However, the first gunship went into its run from the wrong direction and salvoed every rocket on the ship into the B Company CP, killing two members of the company and wounding 14 others, including the company commander. The NVA, seeing the Americans hit by their own rockets, immediately launched a fierce counterattack. During the desperate fighting that ensued, the Americans killed many of the attackers, but in the end, were forced to withdraw. Dennis Helms, Lieutenant Boccia's radio man in the 1st Platoon, several years after the battle, remembered, "That broke our back that day. The battle was bad enough, but having our own gunship fire on us was a hard pill to swallow – it was demoralizing."

On B Company's right flank, A Company made progress until it ran into a strong bunker line. It slugged it out with the NVA, but the death of the platoon sergeant in the lead platoon and other casualties caused the attack to falter. As a thunderstorm broke over their positions, the company had to withdraw, fighting all the way with the pursuing NVA.

Brigade sent Captain Butch Chappel to replace the fallen Littnan in B Company; Lieutenant Lou Charles, a replacement platoon leader, accompanied him. Once on the ground, the new company commander tried to generate a new attack, but B Company, by this time exhausted and suffering from the day's losses, could make no progress.

Honeycutt ordered the two companies to fall back 400m and establish a defensive line for the night. Still at the helicopter crash site from the day before, D Company was also having its problems. With all of his companies back in the original positions where they had spent the previous night, close air support and artillery continued to pound the hill above them.

Honeycutt believed that the Cobra rocketing B Company was the single reason for halting Garza and the 4th Platoon's attack. He sent a message to the division CP saying that he did not want any more armed helicopters in his area if they could not shoot the enemy, rather than his own troops. Moreover, he said, "The next goddam sonofabitch who comes out here and shoots us up, we're gonna shoot his fuckin' ass down."

The troops of 3/187th settled into their NDPs, digging fighting holes, putting out listening posts, and sending out ambush patrols. They also received replacements flown in from Camp Evans. These replacements included cooks, clerks, and other personnel sent from the rear to fill the depleted ranks of the Rakkasans. It had been a tough day, and the new men were desperately needed. A Company had lost 17 men during the day and B Company 19; this left only about half the normal strength of a rifle company. D Company was not in much better shape.

Later that evening, the NVA launched an attack against the 3/187th CP, which was being guarded by C Company. The Americans fended off the attack aided by an AC-119G "Shadow" gunship and its quadruple miniguns, which fired a 24,000-round-a-minute torrent into the attackers. When the "Shadow" expended its ordnance and departed the area, a pair of Cobra gunships continued fire with their miniguns. The decimated NVA continued to fight, but eventually, the soldiers retreated; the Americans sustained one wounded in the action.

Based on the developing situation, Colonel Conmy decided to postpone another attack up Dong Ap Bia until 1/506th was in position to support 3/187th from the south. The new brigade plan called for 3/187th to continue its attack as before up the two ridges, but to hold short of the summit to exert pressure on the NVA defenses while 1/506th assaulted from the west and south to sweep across the top of Hill 900 toward Hill 937.

While waiting for the 506th to get into position, close air support and artillery continued to pound the top and west slope of Dong Ap Bia with every asset that could be mustered. The bombardment began with three sets of fighter-bombers dropping their bombs on the mountaintop. After the jets cleared the area, the artillery on the five supporting firebases poured volley after volley of 105mm, 155mm, and 8in howitzer shells on Dong Ap Bia.

In response to the brigade commander's guidance, Honeycutt ordered Captain Sanders to move D Company back up the main ridge, take over B Company's LZ and prepare to continue the attack. A Company would lead the attack up the adjacent ridge. B Company would move back to the battalion CP and provide security for the battalion headquarters, along with the remnants of C Company. Now Honeycutt just had to wait for 1/506th to keep its end of the bargain.

Medics tend to a wounded trooper who has been felled by an enemy hand grenade while storming Dong Ap Bia on May 18. (Bettmann/Getty Images)

Elsewhere in the brigade area of operations, 2/501st continued its RIF operations in the area surrounding Firebase Airborne. It did not make significant contact with the NVA, but encountered a few small groups that appeared to be trail watchers. At around 1900hrs on the evening of the 15th, Firebase Airborne received six 82mm mortar rounds that did not cause any significant damage.

The 3rd Battalion, 1st ARVN Regiment, also continued operations in its assigned area west of La Dut. During these operations, the South Vietnamese troopers discovered several weapons caches, including an 82mm mortar tube and the graves of about 40 NVA soldiers apparently killed by airstrikes.

Meanwhile, 1/506th continued its advance to the north, but NVA resistance was increasing. The two lead companies, A and C, were moving along separate routes when they both came under heavy fire from fortified bunkers in the vicinity of Hill 916, which was approximately 1km west of Hill 937. Despite the employment of close air support, gunships, and artillery, the NVA clung to its positions, making it increasingly impossible for 1/506th to advance. The two sides battled for the ridgeline for the rest of the 16th.

DAY 8

On May 17, with 1/506th having made little progress, Colonel Conmy again postponed the two-battalion attack up the mountain. Honeycutt was ordered to pull his troops back. While they waited for the arrival of 1/506th, Honeycutt directed his troops to continue preparations for the next assault. They began stockpiling supplies, passing out new protective gas masks, and bringing up concussion grenades for use against the dug-in NVA in the bunkers and trench lines. In preparation for the attack, brigade dropped flak jackets to both 1/506th and 3/187th to help protect their troops against shrapnel wounds to the chest, abdomen, and back regions of the body.

Honeycutt consulted with brigade headquarters, and they decided that on the following day 1/506th and 3/187th would attack simultaneously, which hopefully would force the NVA on Ap Bia to split its available troops. The attack would be preceded by an artillery barrage that would include CS tear gas intended to flush the NVA soldiers out of their spider holes and bunkers. Pink Teams, air cavalry reconnaissance elements consisting of one Loach and one or two Cobra gunships, would screen the area, and airstrikes would be on call.

At about this time, the bitter battle of Dong Ap Bia came to the attention of the media. The Associated Press sent correspondent Jay Sharbutt to investigate the situation. He flew into the LZ on Hill 937 on May 16. After visiting the 3/187th CP and talking with several soldiers in the area, he then flew to Firebase Berchtesgaden, where he met with Major General Zais.

Sharbutt asked Zais, "Why are you attacking this mountain with troops? Why don't you just pull back and hit [Hill 937] with B-52 strikes?" Zais attempted to explain to him that B52s could not be used because of the proximity of American troops to the North Vietnamese positions. However, this failed to mollify the journalist, who was polite but did not buy the general's explanation. Sharbutt's first article appeared in the May 18 issue of *The New York Times*. In the account entitled "Mountain Battle Tough, Bloody for GIs," which was followed by two more, Sharbutt described the bloody battle for Dong Ap Bia. He wrote, "The paratroopers came down the mountain, their green shirts darkened with sweat, their weapons gone, their bandages stained brown and red – with mud and blood." He reported that one of the paratroopers said, "That damn Blackjack [Honeycutt] won't stop until he kills every one of us." Sharbutt's gripping description of the "meat-grinder" battle horrified the American people and set off a firestorm of protest that would go all the way to the floor of Congress.

Wounded soldiers are tended to before being carried to a Huey helicopter for evacuation to the nearest medical facility. (Bettmann/Getty Images)

DAY 9

While this story broke in the States, preparations for the next assault on Dong Ap Bia had been completed. However, by daylight on May 18, 1/506th was still some 500m from Hill 900 and nearly twice that distance from Hill 937. Not wanting to postpone the attack again, Colonel Conmy gave the go-ahead for the coordinated two-battalion assault, with 3/187th attacking from the north and 1/506th attacking from the south. As with the original coordinated attack plan, 3/187th was to push forward until making contact and continue advancing to place maximum pressure on the NVA's defenses. Honeycutt was directed not to get decisively engaged until 1/506th was positioned for its attack up the mountain. Conmy's staff planned airstrikes and artillery to help 1/506th initiate a breakout from its position to get the battalion's attack on the mountain underway to alleviate some of the pressure on 3/187th. It got off to a bad start when the planned fighter-bombers that were to provide airstrikes in support of both 3/187th and 1/506th arrived 30 minutes late. Consequently, the scheduled artillery barrage, meant to begin at 0830hrs, did not start until 0900hrs.

The prep began with the artillery firing CS shells. However, the CS shells missed their target by a quarter of a mile, dumping the gas on A Company, 3/187th. Although the Americans had gas masks, many of their filters had become water-soaked, causing them to malfunction. Dozens of men began to vomit uncontrollably. During the planning for the attack, Honeycutt had requested that CS not be used, but brigade headquarters had overridden him.

A second volley of CS landed on target, but the high winds quickly dispersed it. Specialist Philip Perron, a rifleman from C Company, later recalled, "They figured the NVA would all crawl out of their holes coughing and gagging … [but] the wind shifted and the whole CS gas theory didn't work."

Fortunately for the Americans, the barrage of high explosive shells went better than the CS, falling accurately on NVA positions on the upper slopes of Hill 937. When the artillery lifted at 1025hrs, A and D Companies began their advance up the mountain. By this point, the upper slopes and top of the mountain had been denuded by the continual pounding by artillery and airstrikes. Nevertheless, the NVA clung doggedly to its positions and waited for the Americans to advance.

Honeycutt's troops, wearing flak jackets and heavily laden with grenades and extra rifle ammunition, moved out, heading up the mountain for yet another attempt. For the first 100m, they took only sporadic enemy fire. However, the fighting soon intensified. Progress was slow as gunships, artillery, and mortar fire continued to pound the positions on the summit. At the same time, the men of A and D Companies tried to work their way up the hill against heavy fire.

Confronted by two lines of bunkers, A Company was taking automatic weapons fire, RPGs, and claymore mines from three directions. To make matters worse, the NVA began to drop mortars on the attackers. In the intense fighting, A Company's officers took heavy losses, and the attack completely bogged down.

D Company made more progress at first, but then ran into a bunker line supported by trenches and spider holes. Firing their rifles and M79 grenade launchers, they edged up the mountain against heavy fire. Captain Sanders,

A wounded soldier talks with a chaplain while waiting with other wounded for evacuation. (Bettmann/Getty Images)

the company commander, later recalled, "We burst out of the wood line and [ran into] the most intense fire I have ever seen … incredible, it was very intense."

A secondary explosion caused by a live grenade falling from a dying NVA soldier created a momentary distraction, which Lieutenant Thomas Lipscomb's 2nd Platoon surged forward to exploit. Rushing right up to the bunkers, they fired into their firing slits point blank. Within a few minutes, the Americans overran the bunker line and killed its defenders. By the time they reached the second bunker line, the platoon had suffered six wounded in action. The American troops saw some of the NVA soldiers abandon their positions and try to withdraw up the hill. However, their fire did not slacken. As the 2nd Platoon tried to force its way against the bunker line, a grenade killed Lieutenant Lipscomb and wounded several other soldiers.

Captain Sanders directed Lieutenant Jerry Walden and his 1st Platoon to take the lead and continue the attack up the slope. As they moved forward, they encountered command-detonated MON-100 Soviet claymore mines, one of which seriously wounded Captain Sanders. Lieutenant Walden took over from Sanders, pushing the 1st and 2nd Platoons forward under heavy fire until an NVA heavy machine gun, showers of grenades, and RPG fire halted them. Private First Class Michael Rocklen, a radioman, contacted a FAC circling overhead and requested an airstrike. The FAC called in an A-1 Skyraider and, guided by a smoke grenade Rocklen used to mark his position, the A-1 dropped two canisters of napalm on the NVA position, incinerating a machine-gun position and 30m of trenches. However, D Company was still unable to continue its advance.

Although D Company's progress had been stopped, its attack on the two bunker lines forced the NVA to pull back its troops elsewhere on Hill 937

Soldiers from 3/187th Infantry attack up Dong Ap Bia against heavily entrenched NVA troops. (Bettmann/Getty Images)

American soldiers move through an area where trees have been stripped of their foliage by the bitter fighting in the A Shau Valley. (Bettmann/Getty Images)

to preclude being outflanked and surrounded. Their withdrawal permitted A Company to advance on the battalion's right. Captain Harkins and his troops forced their way through the first line of bunkers and started for the second bunker line. Harkins reported to battalion that he and his men were less than 100m from the top of the hill. However, they soon began to take heavy fire from the ridge on their flank.

B Company sent a platoon toward A Company to take a resupply of ammunition and water for its continued attack up the mountain. However, as they climbed up the slope, a Cobra gunship fired its miniguns at the Americans, killing one and wounding four men. Honeycutt, rightfully enraged, screamed at the pilot on the radio, "Get the fuck out of the area. Do you hear me? Get the fuck out! I don't wanna see any of you incompetent bastards out here the rest of the fight."

The battle continued to rage. D Company almost made it to the top of the hill, but every officer in the company was killed or wounded, and the unit suffered over 50 percent casualties as the battle degenerated into a close-quarters fight, with friendly and enemy troops separated by only a few meters.

Honeycutt ordered C Company to the aid of D Company. However, as C Company, carrying much-needed ammunition for D Company, began to move up the mountain, a blinding rainstorm broke out. The rain turned the slopes into deep mud, making advancement even more difficult. Nevertheless, C Company pushed up the hill; when it reached the first bunker line that D Company had cleared, it discovered that the NVA had reoccupied the positions. Additionally, it was receiving fire from the ridge on its left.

The 1/506th claimed to be on this ridge, but Honeycutt saw the pith helmets of the NVA soldiers there as they fired on his helicopter. It did not appear that the 506th was on the ridgeline in question. Honeycutt radioed it, requesting that it pop smoke to mark its position. It did so, and the smoke revealed it was about 400m away from the ridgeline.

Now certain that 1/560th was not on the ridgeline, Honeycutt called in mortars on the position. On the upper slope of Dong Ap Bia, C Company broke through the NVA bunker line, moved forward, and joined up with the remnants of D Company. Captain Johnson assumed command of the combined C and D force. He began to stabilize the situation, spreading his troops out to cover as much ground as possible.

Honeycutt had concluded that 1/506th was not going to make it to support his attack. He had two companies in contact with the NVA and another moving to join them. He believed that if he eased up on the pressure, the NVA would launch a large counterattack and chop his troops to pieces. To him, there was only one logical option. He called Harkins and Johnson, directing, "Fuck it! We're gonna continue the attack. I'm not gonna turn tail and have you all shot in the back. We're gonna push those bastards off this hill!" Honeycutt thought his troops could take the hill, but he doubted they could hold against a concerted counterattack. He called brigade and requested reinforcements in the form of a new company.

Orbiting over the battlefield in his helicopter, Honeycutt was watching D Company as it tried to get into position. He directed Captain Johnson to maneuver his men up a small finger on his left. Johnson protested that the fire at that location was too heavy, but Honeycutt told him, "Do what I told you!"

Johnson directed Lieutenant Joel Trautman and one of his squads to secure the finger as Honeycutt had ordered. Charging up the hill against intense fire, they advanced from bomb crater to bomb crater, leaping over logs and felled trees. They made it about 30m up the hill when one of his men was wounded. Shortly after that, Trautman, urging his men forward, was shot in the left thigh. When the squad fell back dragging its wounded comrade, Trautman, slipping in and out of consciousness, was left alone as the battle raged around him. He later remembered, "I was up there for [maybe] two hours … I thought I was going to die there." Praying, he decided if the NVA tried to take him captive, he would die fighting and take as many of them with him as he could. Fortunately for him, one of the sergeants in the platoon led a handful of men back up the mountain to rescue the lieutenant. They braved intense fire to get to him. Still under fire, they splinted his leg and, crawling, dragged him back to friendly lines.

Meanwhile, 1/506th was pinned down by a large NVA force in bunkers on the south side of the ridge, Hill 900. Initially, its advance had not been affected by the rain, because the area it was moving through was still covered by thick jungle, not having been pulverized like Hill 937. When the rain let up, it moved forward, but immediately ran into another bunker line. The fighting was slow and deliberate until one of A Company's platoons managed to flank the NVA, and the bunker line was then quickly cleared. With these defenders eliminated, A and B Companies pushed to within 600m of the crest of the hill before digging in for the night.

Flying over Dong Ap Bia, Honeycutt decided to intervene personally to get the attack restarted. He landed at the battalion CP. There he gathered the S3, Major Collier, and his three radio operators and told them to get their weapons and follow him. The group started up the hill on foot to join the attack. It took them 30 minutes to go the 600m to reach the old B Company LZ. He found the area filled with wounded.

After a brief halt to talk with a few men, Honeycutt and his party continued moving up the trail. They had gone barely 100m when they were ambushed by a group of NVA soldiers in a small draw off the trail. A grenade explosion stunned Major Collier, but Honeycutt and the radio operators returned fire, killing six or seven of the NVA. Collier joined the fight, and together the Americans charged into the position, driving off the NVA.

The group continued up the hill to C Company's position. At that point, a tremendous thunderstorm struck the mountain. The downpour turned the red earth into a deep mire, making further movement up the mountain problematic.

By this time, the situation in 3/187th was dire. Casualties had been very heavy, and Honeycutt's companies were all low on ammunition. During the day's fighting, 3/187th had 14 men killed in action and over 60 wounded. Considering that 1/506th had not been able to make sufficient progress up the other side of the hill, Honeycutt concluded that the attack had been effectively stymied. He considered having his troops halt in place and hold until morning, but he was afraid that his exhausted men would not be able to beat back a full counterattack and, in the end, would probably be overrun. There was no alternative except to withdraw and try to get ready for a renewed assault the next morning. He called Colonel Conmy and grudgingly requested permission to pull back.

At 1432hrs, Honeycutt ordered A Company to hold its position and keep a steady stream of fire on the mountain while C and D Companies started pulling back. The withdrawal was orderly, but the North Vietnamese did not let them go easily. The NVA snipers fired at the American troops as they tried to withdraw. C and D Companies fought back with a vengeance, responding with recoilless rifle fire and grenade launchers.

By 1530hrs, most of C and D Companies had withdrawn. As a hard drizzle continued to fall, A Company started its withdrawal. As the last platoon began to pull back, a platoon of NVA charged down the mountain and launched a counterattack. Captain Harkins took charge, turned the platoon around, and met the attackers with rifle and machine-gun fire. This fusillade killed a number of the NVA soldiers and forced the rest to flee back up the mountain.

Major General Zais, who had been monitoring the day's attack from his helicopter overhead, again considered calling off the operation because of the heavy casualties and intense media attention, but he decided to continue

A UH-1H helicopter approaches an LZ; a soldier on the ground has popped smoke to mark the spot. (Bettmann/Getty Images)

A Huey helicopter hovers over a hilltop firebase in the A Shau Valley near the Laotian border as an ARVN soldier looks on. (Bettmann/Getty Images)

the attack. He planned to commit fresh troops to the battle to take the hill. When Zais discussed the new plan with Major General Ngo Quang Truong, commanding general of the 1st ARVN Division, Truong offered a battalion from his 3rd Regiment as part of the reinforcements. Additionally, Zais would insert 2/501st, which had been operating just east of the A Shau Valley, into the fight to take Dong Ap Bia.

During the planning, Zais concluded that the 3/187th was exhausted and too beat up to continue the attack; the battalion had suffered heavily in the repeated assaults up Dong Ap Bia. A and B Companies had lost 50 percent of their original strength; C and D Companies had each suffered 80 percent losses. Two of the four original company commanders in the battalion were killed or wounded, and eight of 12 platoon leaders were casualties, in addition to numerous NCOs. Accordingly, Zais ordered the relief in place of the battered battalion with 2/506th; he did not do this as punishment for failure to take the mountain, but rather to provide respite for the battered Rakkasans.

Shortly after making these decisions, Zais flew to Phu Bai to confer with Lieutenant General Stilwell and the XXIV Corps staff. At Stilwell's CP, Zais was surprised to find Secretary of State William P. Rogers, who was on a fact-finding tour of Vietnam, and General Creighton Abrams, MACV commander, who was accompanying Rogers on his tour. Zais and Abrams discussed the ongoing battle for Dong Ap Bia, and Zais departed Phu Bai to return to his headquarters, confident that he had the backing of both Abrams and Stilwell.

About the same time that Zais was departing Phu Bai, Lieutenant Colonel Gene Sherron, commander of 2/506th, landed at the 3/187th LZ and walked to Honeycutt's CP to coordinate the relief in place. When Sherron told Honeycutt that his battalion had been ordered to relieve the Rakkasans, Honeycutt was incensed. As this conversation unfolded, General Zais landed on the LZ and made his way to the CP. There he told Sherron to get airborne again and then turned to Honeycutt to discuss the new plan.

Honeycutt expressed his outrage at the proposed relief of his battalion by 2/506th, exclaiming in his usual blunt fashion, "I think it stinks, General." Despite his losses, Lieutenant Colonel Honeycutt adamantly protested the relief of his battalion, demanding that his men, who had already paid such a high price, be allowed to continue the mission to take the hill, saying all he needed was one additional company. Honeycutt told his commander,

"General, if there is anybody that deserves to take that sonofabitch, it's the Rakkasans – and you know that as well as I do." Then Honeycutt doubled down, saying, "And if it ain't gonna be that way, then you just better fire my ass right now. Right this minute!" Zais gave in and left 3/187th in the fight, giving Honeycutt A Company from 2/506th for the new attack.

Hovering over the LZ, Sherron got a call from General Smith, the assistant division commander. Smith told him there had been a change of plans and that the 2/506th would not be relieving 3/187th; he also told Sherron to bring in his A Company and put it under the operation control of 3/187th. Sherron was given no reason for the change, but he assumed that Honeycutt had vigorously and successfully protested the original decision.

Troops from 3/187th fire into a North Vietnamese bunker near the top of Dong Ap Bia. (Bettmann/Getty Images)

The brigade plan for the next attack called for 3/187th to hold the NVA in place on the western face of the mountain, while 1/506th and two newly added battalions, 2/501st (from the 2nd Brigade of the 101st Airborne Division) and 2/3rd ARVN, would overrun the summit. Honeycutt again balked, saying:

> We ain't goin' through that fix-the-enemy-in-place routine again. The next time we get to the top of that mountain, we're going to take the sonofabitch. If the 506th gets there, that's fine. And if the 2-501st gets there, it'll be great. And if the ARVN gets there, I will be fucking thrilled. But we ain't gonna sit there like today and get our asses shot off waiting for them.

He promised that the Rakkasans would take the mountain this time, and the brigade concurred with 3/187th pushing to the top of the hill.

In preparation for the renewed attack, 2/501st was picked up by helicopters at Firebase Airborne and inserted into an LZ 800m northeast of Dong Ap Bia. Meanwhile, another fleet of helicopters brought the 2/3rd ARVN to a staging area at Firebase Currahee. From there, it was lifted into an attack position about 1km southeast of Ap Bia, reaching its jumping-off point with no NVA contact.

DAY 10

While these relatively fresh troops arrived, Lieutenant Colonel Bowers and 1/506th began the advance up Hill 900 at 1000hrs on the morning of May 19. With A Company in the lead, the attackers outflanked and destroyed several large clusters of bunkers, killing the NVA inside. They captured the top of

An American soldier fires an M-60 machine gun at enemy positions as he and his comrades attack up Dong Ap Bia. (Bettmann/Getty Images)

the hill at 1300hrs. They found a command post with several documents, including detailed maps of the mountain and the northern A Shau Valley. They also discovered large quantities of ammunition.

With Hill 900 secured, 1/506th pushed on toward Hill 937, but it was quickly pinned down by fire from a large bunker complex. Lieutenant Colonel Bowers directed C Company, which had been following behind A Company to clear by-passed NVA, to swing to the right and try to move up Hill 900 from the southeast to take some of the pressure off A Company.

A mortar crew fires in support of its fellow soldiers attacking Dong Ap Bia. (United States Army Center of Military History)

C Company's commander, Captain William Stymiest, directed Lieutenant Ian Shumaker and 3rd Platoon up a small finger to the left and Lieutenant Timothy LeClair and 2nd Platoon up a small ridge to the right. LeClair and his men followed a minor trail, but it dead-ended at the edge of a small ravine with a small stream running through it. As the men discussed the advisability of crossing the stream into what looked like a perfect place for an ambush, the platoon came under heavy fire. In the ensuing fight, LeClair was shot dead by an NVA soldier. The remainder of the platoon was effectively pinned down by the fire.

On the other finger, Private First Class Paul Skaggs from 3rd Platoon saw the bunkers that had 2nd Platoon pinned down. He moved down the ridge toward the bunkers, armed with a .45 automatic and a satchel stuffed with grenades around his neck. Covered by two men armed with M16s, Skaggs moved to the first bunker. He threw several grenades into the bunker and, after the grenades exploded, he killed the NVA inside with his pistol. He repeated this again and again until he had wiped out the four remaining bunkers. With this line of resistance eliminated, both platoons resumed their advance to their assigned assault positions, where they set up a defensive perimeter for the night and prepared for the next day's coordinated attack.

Meanwhile, Honeycutt had gathered all his company commanders and they flew over the battlefield for a commander's recon. Once back at the CP, Honeycutt laid out the plan for the next day's attack. C Company would be the main effort, attacking up the main ridgeline leading to the summit. A Company would parallel C Company with an attack up the southern spur. A Company, 2nd/506th, commanded by Captain Bill Womble, would follow C Company initially, before swinging to the left to protect C Company's left flank. D Company would be the battalion reserve and initially follow A Company, 2/506th. B Company was responsible for securing the battalion CP and bringing forward ammunition and other supplies when needed.

Atop Hill 937, the North Vietnamese soldiers also prepared for the next day's battle. During the evening, a North Vietnamese hailed Honeycutt on a captured American radio. He warned, "When you come up the mountain in the morning, Blackjack, we will be waiting for you. All of your men are going to die. Can you hear me, Blackjack? All will die!" Undaunted, Honeycutt snapped, "We'll see who dies tomorrow, asshole!"

FINAL ASSAULT

At 0530hrs on May 20, 3/187th began its morning with a stand-to. All along the battalion perimeter, the men ripped the surrounding jungle with rifle and machine-gun fire hoping to catch any NVA soldiers who might have crept close during the night.

At 0630hrs, as if in response, the North Vietnamese launched several small attacks of their own. In one instance, a squad of NVA soldiers fired several RPGs at the battalion CP; a platoon from B Company returned fire, but the NVA withdrew.

About 30 minutes later, an NVA soldier approached A Company, 2/506th, with a grenade in his hand with the pin pulled. He was trying to breach the perimeter, but the defenders riddled him with rifle fire when he was about 15m away. When he fell, the grenade exploded on top of him.

On the southeastern side of the mountain, an NVA soldier wearing a rucksack approached the perimeter of A Company, 1/506th, with his hands up, yelling in English that he wished to surrender. When he reached within 10m of the Americans, he detonated a claymore mine in his backpack, blowing himself up and badly wounding four US soldiers.

At 1000hrs on May 20, after ten artillery batteries fired more than 20,000 rounds and 272 tactical airstrikes dumped over a million pounds of bombs and 152,000lb of napalm virtually denuded the top of the mountain, the coordinated brigade attack began. Once again, 3/187th started up the mountain, supported by 1/506th, which renewed its attack on the southern side, while 2/501st attacked from the northeast and 2/3rd ARVN advanced from the southeast.

Honeycutt's three companies started up the mountain on three separate axes: A Company on the right, C Company in the center, and A Company,

2/506th, on the far left. They expected to encounter the same withering fire that they had experienced since the beginning of the fight for Dong Ap Bia, but it was strangely quiet. The attackers hoped it meant that the NVA had abandoned its positions and withdrawn into Laos during the night. They pushed upward, using grenades and satchel charges to destroy or seal the bunkers they encountered. As they advanced, the attackers found a hellish landscape characterized by torn earth and jungle still burning from the effects of the artillery and airstrikes.

As the converging troops from 3/187th got closer to the top of Hill 937, they encountered a bunker line ringing the crest, but it was deserted. They destroyed the bunkers and continued their advance. At this point, C Company was hit with rifle, machine-gun, and RPG fire from the surviving defenders in a second line of several large, A-frame bunkers, which had been too strong for the airstrikes and artillery to destroy. Seven C Company soldiers were wounded, but the company returned fire. The NVA then rolled grenades down the hill, wounding four more men from C Company.

With 75m to go to the top of the hill, Honeycutt, orbiting the battlefield in an OH-6 helicopter, urged his troops onward. However, C Company was pinned down. Honeycutt screamed, "Use the 90mm! Knock those fucking bunkers out!" Captain Johnson called for his recoilless rifle team. Specialist Fourth Class Tyrone Campbell and his assistant gunner rushed forward. Taking cover behind a log, Campbell fired at the bunker, which exploded. He kept at it, moving down the line, firing at the bunkers in turn, taking out three.

On C Company's right flank, Specialist Fourth Class Edward Merjil, from 2nd Platoon, knocked out two bunkers by firing M79 rounds directly into their firing slits. The men of 2nd Platoon, C Company, 3/187th, rushed forward. It was 1145hrs, and they became the first Americans to reach the summit of Dong Ap Bia, exactly nine days and five hours after B Company first made contact on the mountain.

Immediately above the battle in his OH-6, Honeycutt saw 2nd Platoon take out the bunkers, but realized that it was alone with the NVA still dug in to its right and left. He was worried that the NVA might counterattack and push C Company off the hill. However, as he watched, the rest of C Company arrived on the mountaintop and methodically began to blow up the remaining bunkers. He saw the NVA begin to desert its positions and run down the west side of the mountain, through the saddle between Hill 937 and Hill 904, toward the safety of Laos.

Honeycutt called in fires from his 81mm mortar platoon, then called Lieutenant Colonel Bowers and asked him to block the enemy escape route. Bowers directed his B Company to take out the fleeing soldiers. The retreating NVA ran into rifle and machine-gun fire from the B Company troopers; about ten NVA soldiers were killed in the first volley, but the survivors quickly regrouped and

US soldiers inspect the damage in the surrounding area of Dong Ap Bia in the aftermath of the battle. (United States Army Center of Military History)

Final assault, May 20, 1969

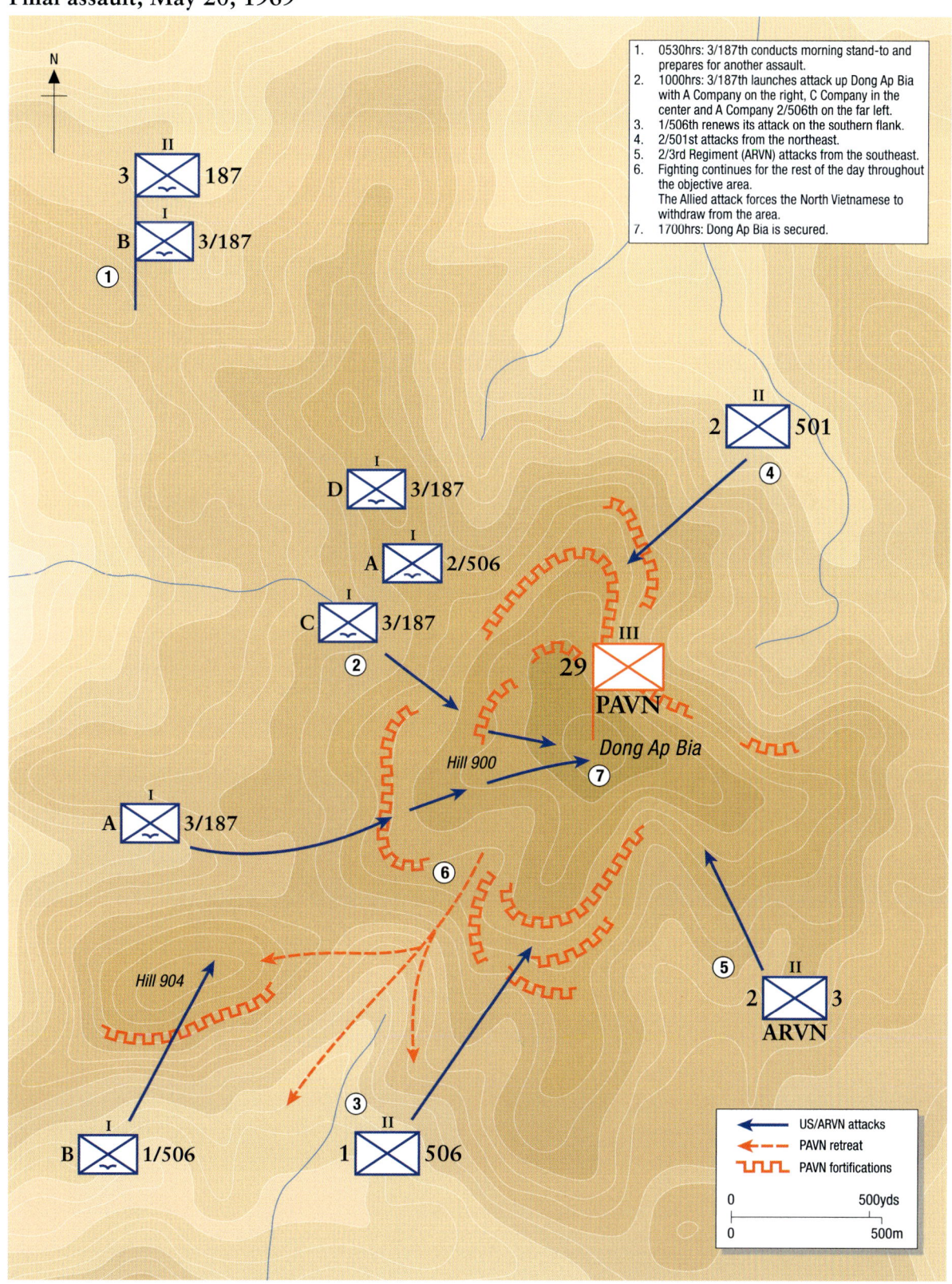

FINAL ASSAULT ON DONG AP BIA, MAY 20, 1969 (PP.82–83)

A and C Companies from 3/187th launch what turns out to be the final assault to take Dong Ap Bia. The terrain was a steep slope leading to the top of Hill 937 (**1**); it had been blasted by almost continuous artillery and repeated airstrikes. The Americans attacking up the hill are armed with M-16 rifles (**2**) and M-60 machine guns (**3**) and grenades. The North Vietnamese soldiers from the 29th Regiment of the NVA man bunkers and firing positions, firing down the mountain toward the attackers with AK-47s, RPD machine guns, RPGs, and hand-thrown grenades. Overhead is an OH-6 light observation helicopter (**4**), from which the battalion commander monitors the progress of the battle.

Starting at 1000hrs after a preparatory bombardment by close air support and artillery, C Company leads the attack up the main ridgeline leading to the summit while A Company attacks on the right. A/2/506th attached to 3/187th follows C Company initially and then swings left to protect C Company's left flank. During the attack, Specialist Fourth Class Johnny Jackson from A Company, armed with an M-60 machine gun, dashes up the mountain firing from the hip (**5**). This galvanizes the Americans and they surge up the mountain. The US troops advance through successive enemy bunker lines while taking intense enemy fire.

A US Army photographer and his assistant climb through the devastated landscape on Dong Ap Bia after the battle. (United States Army Center of Military History)

counterattacked. A sharp fight ensued, but the men from B Company held the line. For the next two hours, they would engage group after group of NVA soldiers pouring off the mountain, trying to escape to Laos.

With C Company at the top, but in a precarious position, A Company was dealing with its own fight as it tried to move through the second bunker line against heavy NVA fire, sustaining 16 wounded, including a platoon leader. As the company tried to push through the NVA resistance, Captain Harkins, the company commander, was seriously wounded when a bullet passed through his left ear and neck, lodging in his back. Harkins, unable to hear and having lost sight in one eye, directed his radio man to move up the hill while he held onto the radio to maintain his balance. The NVA increased its fire and again rolled grenades down the slope, stalling A Company's attack.

Several individuals reenergized the A Company attack. Specialist Fourth Class Johnny Jackson, an M-60 gunner in 3rd Platoon, yelled, "Fuck this bullshit!" and dashed forward, spraying bullets in every direction as he leaped over logs and other debris. He made it to a shell crater, but was wounded by a white phosphorus marking rocket fired by a FAC flying over the mountain. Nevertheless, he held his position, effectively securing A Company's south flank. However, he was now pinned down by fire from a dozen NVA soldiers in a nearby trench line.

Watching Jackson's charge, Specialist Fourth Class Michael Vallone yelled, "Follow me … Come on, everybody, follow me!" Galvanized by Vallone's charge, the men of A Company, first his squad, then all of 3rd Platoon, and then the rest of the company surged forward and seized the top of the hill. Captain Harkins followed with the aid of his radio man. At the top of the hill, Harkins quickly organized a defensive perimeter, tying in with C Company. He then collapsed; Lieutenant Gordie Atcheson took command of the company. At about the time this occurred, A Company, 2/506th also seized

A lone US soldier surveys the devastation after battle. (Bettmann/Corbis/Getty Images)

the northern portion of the hill and secured C Company's northern flank.

The Rakkasans from A and C Companies atop the hill continued to take heavy small-arms fire from the west and RPG and small-arms fire from the south as the NVA tried to cover its withdrawal. The 3/187th troopers were not to be denied and returned fire with M16s, machine guns, M79 grenade launchers, and 90mm recoilless rifles while calling in artillery and gunships to hit the fleeing North Vietnamese. While the other battalions continued toward their assigned objectives, 3/187th cleared out the last enemy resistance, finding some 78 dead NVA and capturing one prisoner of war. It also found a burial trench with over 100 bodies.

The American troops discovered that the hill was honeycombed with tunnels and trenches. They discovered a room in one of the tunnels with 40 dead NVA soldiers stacked like cordwood. They also found a functional hospital and a storage room with 75,000 rounds of ammunition, thousands of mortar rounds and RPGs, and over 10 tons of rice.

While 3/187th cleared the remaining pockets of resistance on the hill, 1/506th continued to fight its way forward, encountering heavy small-arms, RPG, and mortar fire. After several hard-fought battles, the battalion's companies had cleaned out numerous bunkers and prevailed in several close-in firefights, reaching the southern edge of the mountain at about 1500hrs, where they dug in for the night.

Pushing up the northeast side of Dong Ap Bia, 2/501st had an easier time. It encountered only light resistance and a series of bunkers vacated by the retreating NVA.

Meanwhile, what became a very controversial aspect of the battle of Hamburger Hill unfolded. Attacking from the southeast, 2nd Battalion, 3rd ARVN Regiment, commanded by Lieutenant Colonel Pham Van Dinh, had launched its attack early and initially encountered light resistance, discovering several ammunition caches and several abandoned bunker complexes along the way. As the South Vietnamese soldiers neared the top of the hill, they began to receive concentrated small-arms fire. They called in artillery and close air support, killing or driving off the NVA. The ARVN continued the advance toward the top of Dong Ap Bia. The battalion's lead elements reached the crest at 1000hrs and the ARVN troops began to consolidate their positions and arrange for evacuation of three killed in action and five wounded soldiers.

Colonel Conmy and Colonel Phan Van Hoa, commander of the 3rd Regiment of the 1st ARVN Division, along with Colonel Hoa's US adviser, Lieutenant Colonel Cecil Fair, were in a helicopter circling above the battle. Fair reported to Conmy that the crest of the mountain was in ARVN hands and that 2/3rd awaited orders.

According to historian Andrew Wiest, Conmy told Fair "to get your people [the ARVN] off the hill, because we are going to fire an artillery preparation on top of the hill." Conmy then called in a fire mission to facilitate the ongoing Rakkasan attack. A frustrated Hoa gave the order, and his men moved back down the hill. After the 3/187th took the hill, the ARVN returned to the top.

US soldiers rest atop the denuded crest of Hamburger Hill after the ten-day battle. (Associated Press/Alamy Stock Photo)

This whole issue remains contentious. Some claim the South Vietnamese were the first to reach the top of Dong Ap Bia. Several historical documents support this claim. However, others are adamant that 3/187th achieved the final victory, reaching the crest first. When historian Wiest asked Honeycutt via telephone about the claim that the South Vietnamese troops got there first, Honeycutt vehemently responded, "There were no goddamned ARVN within a mile of that goddamned hill."

This controversy aside, at the end of the day, US and ARVN soldiers had taken Dong Ap Bia and driven the North Vietnamese troops back into Laos. The victors spent the rest of the day cleaning out the remaining NVA from the bunkers and trenches. When a squad from A Company spotted a group of NVA in a cluster of trees near the center of the mountain, they took them under fire, killing eight soldiers. When they examined the bodies, they found that four of the men had been chained to a tree, apparently to show their willingness to die. All the dead had small cloth patches sewn to their shirts that said, "KILL AMERICANS." Several exhortations had been scribbled on what was left of one of the shattered trees. One read, "DEFEAT THE AMERICANS, HERE WE TAKE A STAND." Another said, "STAY AND FIGHT AND NOT RUN."

By 1700hrs, the battle for Dong Ap Bia was over. What had been won was a hellish landscape marked by shattered trees, destroyed bunkers, bomb craters, broken weapons, scattered equipment, and many North Vietnamese bodies. The North Vietnamese had paid a horrible price to defend Dong Ap Bia and a major base area had been neutralized. However, taking the mountain had also been costly for the victors, and the battle would become one of the most controversial of the entire conflict, ultimately contributing to changing the course of the war.

AFTERMATH

A short time after Dong Ap Bia was secured, a trooper cut out the cardboard bottom of a C-ration box, printed "Hamburger Hill" on it, and tacked it to a charred tree trunk near the western edge of Hill 937. Another soldier, passing by, added the words, "Was it worth it?" This was a very good question.

Using MACV's usual measure of effectiveness, the battle for Hamburger Hill had been a victory. More than 600 North Vietnamese bodies were found on the hill when the battle was over. A prisoner of war captured during the operation indicated that 80 percent of the men in his unit were casualties. Aside from the bodies strewn about the mountain, it will never be known just how many North Vietnamese soldiers were killed and wounded and were carried into Laos or were buried in collapsed bunkers and tunnels on the mountain. A US Special Forces patrol on the Laotian side of the border later reported some 1,100 NVA dead and wounded being removed from the hill during the battle.

When the Rakkasans searched the top of the mountain, they discovered a network of tunnels connecting a large hospital, a regimental command post, and numerous large storage areas full of various weapons and rice.

Even considering the number of NVA killed and the materiel and equipment destroyed or captured, the taking of Dong Ap Bia had been a costly affair. The 3/187th suffered 36 dead and 305 wounded; the total US casualties for the operation were 72 killed and 372 wounded, not counting the losses at Firebase Airborne. South Vietnamese losses for the battle included 31 killed in action.

General Zais regretted the loss of American lives, but was pleased with the overall result of the battle. The 7th and 8th Battalions of the 29th NVA Regiment were virtually wiped out in the battle. An after-action report noted that "the 29th North Vietnamese Army Regiment had been eliminated as a force to contend with at a later date." To Zais, the battle had never been for terrain, but rather to find and destroy enemy forces; from that perspective, the battle was a success.

On May 21, the day following the capture of the summit, 3/187th, which had borne the brunt of the fighting throughout the battle for Hill 937, was extracted from the base of the mountain and helicoptered to Firebase Blaze, where it became OPCON to 2nd Brigade. Following a short respite at Blaze, it was flown to Eagle Beach, a division R&R Center on the South China Sea for much-needed rest and recuperation. MACV rotated Honeycutt and all other surviving officers out of command within a month, which was the standard MACV procedure of rotating combat commanders every six months.

Operation *Apache Snow* continued with US and South Vietnamese troops remaining in the area after Dong Ap Bia was taken, clearing and destroying bunkers, searching for weapons and supplies, and eliminating the North Vietnamese soldiers still in the area. The 2/501st pursued the NVA west to the Laotian border turning north and then back to the east. By this point, the NVA appeared no longer interested in maintaining contact. Operation *Apache Snow* was discontinued on June 7.

Back in the United States, the battle had become very controversial. The fact that the American troops had prevailed in the desperate struggle made little impact on the outrage that had developed at home in the wake of Jay Sharbutt's newspaper accounts of the battle. In the US Senate on May 20, Edward Kennedy of New York angrily denounced the attack on Dong Ap Bia, charging that it was "both senseless and irresponsible to continue to send our young men to their deaths to capture hills and positions that have no relation to this conflict." He proclaimed it "madness … symptomatic of a mentality and a policy that requires immediate attention. American boys are too valuable to be sacrificed to a false sense of military pride."

Senator Edward M. Kennedy (left), D-Mass, at a meeting of the Senate Democratic Policy Committee; in a speech on the Senate floor later, Kennedy criticized the military for "senseless, and irresponsible" pride that led to the bloody battles like "Hamburger Hill." (Bettmann/Getty Images)

On May 24, Kennedy continued his tirade in a speech to the New Democratic Coalition in Washington, calling the battle nothing but "cruelty and savagery" and the war in Vietnam unjustified and immoral. Kennedy denounced President Nixon's Vietnam policy, declaring such operations as those in the A Shau Valley as "counter to our stated goals and intentions in Paris [at the ongoing peace negotiations]." Nixon had been elected, at least in part, because he promised to end the war and achieve "peace with honor." Looking at the casualty figures for the battle, Operation *Apache Snow* and the fight for Dong Ap Bia appeared to be the same old "business as usual." It looked like the usual meat grinder that resulted in a great loss of American lives that contributed nothing toward ending the war.

Kennedy was soon joined by other senators, including South Dakota's George S. McGovern, a decorated World War II bomber pilot, and Ohio's Stephen M. Young. On May 29, Young, who had served as an artilleryman in World War I and an Army staff officer in World War II, vilified the generals in Vietnam for "fling[ing] our paratroopers piecemeal in frontal assaults. Instead of seeking to surround the enemy and seeking to assault the fill from the sides and the front simultaneously, there was one frontal assault after another, killing our boys who went up Hamburger Hill."

Major General Zais was stunned by the reaction at home. He told his officers, "These people are acting like this was a catastrophe for the US troops." At a news conference in Phu Bai, he explained the rationale for the attack on Hill 937, saying bluntly, "That was where the enemy was, and that was where I attacked him." Additionally, insisting that the battle had been a "tremendous, gallant victory," Zais said he had received no change in mission and that the battle for Ap Bia was in keeping with the guidance to exert "maximum pressure" on the enemy.

After the battle, Zais, who had been previously scheduled to relinquish his command, was replaced by Major General John Wright. The new commander subsequently gave the order on June 5 to abandon Dong Ap Bia.

President Richard Nixon and South Vietnam President Nguyen Van Thieu and aides discuss the withdrawal of US troops from Vietnam at the Midway conference in June 1969. (Bettmann/Getty Images)

The controversy over "Hamburger Hill" only increased when military intelligence reported two weeks later that more than 1,000 North Vietnamese troops had moved back into the area and reoccupied Dong Ap Bia as soon as the US and ARVN forces withdrew.

The withdrawal of the allied forces from Dong Ap Bia only added fuel to the public outrage over the bloody fighting there. In the Senate, Kennedy was further incensed, asking, "How can we justify sending our boys against a hill a dozen times, finally taking it, and then withdrawing a week later?"

The media also continued to react. An article in *The New York Times* declared that "the public is certainly entitled to raise questions about the current aggressive posture of the United States military in South Vietnam." The situation was made worse when the June 27, 1969, issue of *Life* magazine featured photographs of the 242 servicemen killed in Vietnam the previous week, including those who had died in the fight for Hamburger Hill during that period. The feature was titled "The Faces of the Dead in Vietnam: One Week's Toll." The article was prefaced by a quote from a letter written by one of the soldiers who died on Hamburger Hill: "You may not be able to read this. I am writing in a hurry. I see death coming up the hill." This contributed to an erroneous perception among many Americans that all 242 pictured died during the Hamburger Hill assault, increasing public disgust over what appeared to be a senseless loss of life.

The battle for Dong Ap Bia came at a time when the support for the war was on a steeply downward path. A February 1969 poll revealed that only 39 percent of the American people still supported the war, while 52 percent believed sending troops to fight in Vietnam had been a mistake. The battle, while a tactical success in keeping the North Vietnamese off balance in I Corps, resulted in a public outcry against the seemingly meaningless nature of the struggle, which resulted in such a bloody expenditure of lives only to have US forces abandon the battlefield shortly after the fighting was over.

The battle of Hamburger Hill symbolized to many the frustration of winning costly battles without ever consummating a strategic victory. The battle had been won but at a very high price, only to be abandoned for the Communists to reoccupy. Giving up such hard-won territory seemed to typify the purposelessness of the war and, to many Americans, served as a symbol of the new Nixon administration's failure to make any substantive changes to the American approach in Vietnam, despite his vows to end the war made during the 1968 presidential election.

The controversial battle ultimately contributed to a reappraisal of US strategy in the Vietnam War. Officials from the Nixon administration admitted to Hedrick Smith of *The New York Times* that such costly victories would further undermine public support for the war and thus shorten the administration's time for successful negotiations in Paris. The public outcry against the seemingly senseless bloodshed at Hamburger Hill appears to have had an impact on deliberations in the Nixon administration about the way ahead in the war. If the president was going to have time to achieve "peace with honor" as he had promised, he had to make sure there were no more

Hamburger Hills. Accordingly, he gave explicit orders to General Abrams that he was subsequently to "conduct the war with a minimum of American casualties."

Shortly after that, at a conference with President Nguyen Van Thieu on Midway Island in June, Nixon announced that he intended to "Vietnamize" the war. The responsibility for fighting would gradually be shifted to the South Vietnamese forces, and concurrent with that effort, the US would begin withdrawing troops from Vietnam. He subsequently announced that the first contingent of 25,000 US troops would depart for home by the end of August.

On August 15, 1969, General Abrams received a new mission statement for MACV that charged him to focus his efforts on assisting the South Vietnamese armed forces "to take over an increasing share of combat operations." Moreover, MACV was to assist the Republic of Vietnam "in assuming full responsibility for the planning and execution of national security and development programs at the earliest feasible date."

Vietnam veteran Colonel Harry Summers best summed up the impact of the battle of Hamburger Hill in a June 1999 article in *Vietnam* magazine, writing:

> The expenditure of effort at Hamburger Hill exceeded the value the American people attached to the war in Vietnam. The public had turned against the war a year and a half earlier, and their intense reaction to the cost of the battle in American lives, inflamed by sensationalist media reporting, forced the Nixon administration to order the end of major tactical ground operations.

Hamburger Hill proved to be the last campaign in Westmoreland's discredited attrition strategy and it was also the final battle in which the outcome was determined by enemy body count. As Summers observed, "The battle spelled finish to large-scale US Army and Marine Corps offensive engagements in the war and was the culmination of major US ground combat operations in Vietnam." Before Hamburger Hill, senior US commanders were still seeking victory on the battlefield; after Hamburger Hill, they were only seeking a way out.

A still from *Hamburger Hill*, a 1987 movie about the battle directed by John Irvin. (Sunset Boulevard/Getty Images)

The first contingent of US soldiers to depart Vietnam in the wake of the Midway Conference board a C-141 Starlifter at Tan Son Nhut International Airport in July 1969. (The Asahi Shimbun/Getty Images)

THE BATTLEFIELD TODAY

Although Dong Ap Bia remains remote today, groups of visitors and veterans, many of whom fought there, still return to the site of the bloody battle. Several travel companies will provide a guide for a trip to the battle area. For those making the trip, the best place to begin is Hue, which offers good hotels and serves as a jumping-off point for a journey west to the A Shau Valley. The trip to the site of the battle by car or bus along Route 49 takes about two hours one way. On the way toward the Laotian border where Dong Ap Bia is located, travelers can stop by the sites of several firebases such as Birmingham, Checkmate, and Bastogne. However, there is not much left to see at these sites. Continuing west, travelers must stop at the village of A Luoi to show the proper travel permits, which can be obtained from the travel company. There is also a small museum there.

Once in the area, there is a path of about a kilometer's climb that guides use, which approaches Ap Bia from the southeast past Hill 900 and up to a monument built by the local government. The path is steep, with a large number of steps installed to negotiate the steeper parts of the trail, but the steps are in poor condition, making it a challenging climb.

The memorial at the top of Hill 900 has signs in Vietnamese and English. Propaganda-laden, these signs describe the battle as a victory for the North Vietnamese and how this place became an "obsession" for US forces. They tell how the Vietnamese "defeated America-quisling's raids, wiped out many enemy army groups, contributed to our country's victory in the resistance war against America." These statements are similar to other such pronouncements encountered in war museums and battle sites throughout Vietnam.

From the memorial, visitors can continue up the trail to the summit of Hill 937, which is about 500m north. It is a demanding hike uphill through heavy jungle and elephant grass. The temperature is always hot and can be particularly unpleasant on the path to the summit when it leaves the cover of the tall trees and subjects the visitors to the sun's full heat. Depending on the time of the visit, there can also be rainstorms that can make trafficability problematic. The steep

The memorial at the top of Dong Ap Bia in 2023. (© Bethany Myers Railing)

climb requires a significant level of physical fitness to complete.

For those who decide to take the trail, there are a few signs along the way pointing to sites nearby where events took place during the battle, including a helicopter crash, bomb craters, and several fortifications. There is also the site of an NVA hospital during the battle. There is a sign at the summit, but it is in Vietnamese.

Across the summit is a trail leading to the right (north) to a ridge where first B Company and later D Company fought their way up. Further exploration of the summit reveals the downward-sloping ridge from which A Company's final attack came. It is very steep, and the jungle cover is very dense.

There is not much evidence remaining of the bitter fighting that happened on Hill 937. Local villagers dug up this and other old battle sites looking for scrap metal to sell. However, if visitors look closely as they move through the jungle, they will see old tree trunks pockmarked by bullet holes and large puddles of water in bomb or artillery craters. Occasionally, one can see evidence of trench lines and even small squared-out holes, called "spider holes," by the US troops who fought there. More than likely, these camouflaged openings led to an underground network of tunnels and storage areas.

For those visitors who wish to, they can also go up the eastern side of the mountain, but the most sustained fighting and the initial LZ were to the west, nearer Laos. In 2014, when historian James Wright visited the mountain, the west side did not have a road or trail, and the Vietnamese guides warned him and his party to avoid that area because of unexploded ordnance. This is true of many battle sites that can be visited today.

Having visited Dong Ap Bia, a side trip can be arranged to the site of the A Shau Special Forces Camp on the Laotian border that was overrun by the NVA in 1966. Visitors can still see several bomb craters from B52 aircraft.

The trip to Dong Ap Bia in the remote area near the Laotian border is a bit out of the way for the casual visitor to Vietnam. The hike up the mountain to the summit will take at least half a day. For those travelers who want to explore the area fully, it is recommended that they consider spending the night before in a hotel in A Luoi to get an early start tackling the mountain before the temperature becomes too hot. All of that being said, it is well worth the effort to see where the bitter battle of Hamburger Hill took place in May 1969.

Steps to the memorial on Dong Ap Bia in 2023. (© Bethany Myers Railing)

A sign warning about the cleared path and the possibility of the presence of unexploded ordnance on Dong Ap Bia in 2023. (© Bethany Myers Railing)

FURTHER READING

Books

Boccia, Frank, *The Crouching Beast: A United States Army Lieutenant's Account of the Battle for Hamburger Hill*, May 1969 (McFarland & Company, Inc., 2013)

Daddis, Gregory A., *Withdrawal: Reassessing America's Final Years in Vietnam* (Oxford University Press, 2017)

Davidson, Phillip B., *Vietnam at War: The History 1946–1975* (Oxford University Press, 1988)

Diconsiglio, John, *Vietnam: Blood Bath at Hamburger Hill* (Franklin Watts, 2009)

Dunstan, Simon and Michael Sharpe, *Elite Attack Forces: Airborne in Vietnam* (Chartwell Books, 2007)

Hammond, William M., *Reporting Vietnam: Media & Military at War* (University Press of Kansas, 1998)

Lipsman, Samuel and Edward Doyle, *Fighting for Time* (*The Vietnam Experience*) (Boston Publishing Company, 1984)

Phillips, Jay, *A Shau: Crucible of the Vietnam War* (Izzard Ink Publishing, 2021)

Rothman, Gordon L., *US Army Infantryman in Vietnam 1965–73* (Osprey Publishing, 2005)

Smith, Charles R., *US Marines in Vietnam: High Mobility and Standdown 1969* (History and Museums Division Headquarters, US Marine Corps, 1988)

Sorley, Lewis, *A Better War: The Unexamined Victories and Final Tragedy of America's Last Years in Vietnam* (Harcourt Brace, 1999)

Sorley, Lewis, ed., *Vietnam Chronicles: The Abrams Tapes, 1968–1972* (Texas Tech University Press, 2004)

Spector, Ronald H., *After Tet: The Bloodiest Year in Vietnam* (The Free Press, 1993)

Wiest, Andrew, *Vietnam's Forgotten Army: Heroism and Betrayal in the ARVN* (NYU Press, 2007)

Wiknik, Arthur, *Nam Sense: Surviving Vietnam with the 101st Airborne Division* (Casemate, 2005)

Willbanks, James H., *Abandoning Vietnam: How America Left and South Vietnam Lost Its War* (University Press of Kansas, 2004)

Woodruff, Mark, *Unheralded Victory: The Defeat of the Viet Cong and the North Vietnamese Army, 1961–1973* (Presidio Press, 2005)

Yarborough, Thomas, *A Shau Valor: American Combat Operations in the Valley of Death, 1963–1971* (Casemate, 2016)

Zaffiri, Samuel, *Hamburger Hill, May 11–20, 1969* (Presidio Press, 1988)

Online Sources

Battle of Hamburger Hill Virtual Staff Ride, Army University Press, Fort Leavenworth, Kansas (www.armyupress.army.mil/Staff-Rides/Virtual-Staff-Ride/Hamburger-Hill-Vietnam-Virtual-Staff-Ride/).

Headquarters, 101st Airborne Division (Airmobile) Operational Report – Lessons Learned, 101st Airborne Division (Airmobile) for Period Ending 31 July 1969, dated August 20, 1969 (https://apps.dtic.mil/sti/tr/pdf/AD0506515.pdf).

Headquarters 101st Airborne Division, Fact Sheet: Summary of Action and Results, Operation Apache Snow, dated May 24, 1969 (https://web.archive.org/web/20190515114632/https://www.vietnam.ttu.edu/star/images/1683/168300010494.pdf).

Headquarters 3d Brigade, 101st Airborne Division (Airmobile), Combat Operations After Action Report Summary – APACHE SNOW, dated June 25, 1969 (https://www.2ndbde.org/archives/after_action_reports/operation_apache_snow_hq_3bde_25_june_1969.pdf).

Vietnam Studies, War in the Northern Provinces, 1966–68, by Lieutenant General Willard Pearson, Department of the Army, Washington, D.C., 1991 (https://history.army.mil/html/books/090/90-24/index.html).

INDEX

Figures in **bold** refer to illustrations.

A Shau Valley 7–9, **7**, **8**
Abrams, General Creighton W. 6, **6**, 12, 76
Addison, Captain Charles 45, 46
Airborne, Firebase 37, 38, 51–52, 69
aircraft, fixed-wing
    A-1E Skyraider 44
    AC-47 "Spooky" gunship 49, **49**, 50, 52–53, 54
    AC-119G "Shadow" gunship 68
    B-52 Stratofortress 35
    C-141 Starlifter 91
    F-4 Phantom 56
    OV-10 Bronco 37
Ap Bia, Dong
    described 7, 7–8, 57, 66–67, 92–93
    final assault on 79–87, **80**, **81**, **82–83**, **84**, **85**, **86**, **87**
    today 92, 92–93, **93**
Apache Snow, Operation 6, 13, 33–34, 88–89
Army of the Republic of Vietnam (ARVN) **26**, 27–28
    2/1st Regt 38
    3/1st Regt 11, 38, 69
    4/1st Regt 38
    2/3rd Regt 77, 86–87
    3/3rd Regt 13
    Hac Bao Recon Co 10, **12**
Atcheson, Lieutenant Gordie 85

Barski, Sergeant Roger 55
Base Area 611: 7, 46
Berchtesgaden, Firebase 37
Blaze, Firebase 34, 37
Boccia, Lieutenant Frank 21, 45–46, 50, 62, 63
Bowers, Lieutenant Colonel James 22, 77
Bradley, Firebase 37
Bruschette, Captain Jerome 9

Campbell, Specialist Tyrone 80
Cannon, Firebase 37
casualties, final 88
chaplains **60**, 72
Chappel, Captain Butch 68
Charles, Lieutenant Lou 68
chronology, battle 14–16
Civilian Irregular Defense Group (CIDG) 9
close air support 37
Collier, Major John 47, 74–75
Conmy, Colonel Joseph B. 19–20, 43, 55, 86
Counts, Sergeant Kenneth 55
Culkin, Lieutenant Colonel Thomas J. 22
Currahee, Firebase 37, 77

Da Krong River 7

Davis, Lieutenant Colonel Donald 22
Delaware, Operation **10**, 10–11
DeLoach, Lieutenant Colonel William W. 22
Denholm, Lieutenant Charles 46, 47
Dewey Canyon, Operation **11**, 12–13
Dien Bien Phu 5
Dinh, Lieutenant Colonel Pham Van 22–23, 86
Doi, Senior Colonel Chu Phuong 23, 35

Eagle Beach R&R Center 88
evacuation, medical 47, 48, 58, 59, **59**, 70
Eward, Lieutenant Marshall 50, 56–58
exit strategy, US 6

Fair, Lieutenant Colonel Cecil 86
flak jackets 70
forward air control 51
Fox, Lieutenant Colonel George C. 22
friendly fire incidents 47, 64, 68, 73

Gann, Private Terry 45
Garza, Sergeant Louis 47, 61, 63, 68
Giap, General Vo Nguyen 36
Goff, Lieutenant 61

Hamburger Hill *see* Ap Bia, Dong
Hamburger Hill (movie) 91
Harkins, Captain Gerald 48, 75, 85
helicopters
    AH-1 Cobra 27, 45
    CH-34: 9
    CH-47 Chinook 35
    OH-6 Cayuse 'Loach' 39, 83, 84
    UH-1H Huey 9, 12, **36**, 48, 75, 76
Helms, Trooper Dennis 45, 68
Hill 900: 61–62, **67**, 71–74, 77–78, **81**
Hill 937 *see* Ap Bia, Dong
Ho Chi Minh 5, 31
Ho Chi Minh Trail 7, **27**
Hoa, Colonel Phan Van 22, 86
Honeycutt, Lieutenant Colonel Weldon F. **20**, 20–21, 38–39, 43, 46–49, 59–76, 87
Hue city 10
Hyde, Private Nate 46

Ia Drang Valley, battle of 34–35
Indochina War, First 5
initial insertions 37–43, **39**, **40–41**, 42

Jackson, Specialist Johnny **82**, 84, 85
Johnson, Captain Dean 48, 61, 62–63, 74
Johnson, Captain Gordon C. 51
Johnson, President Lyndon B. 5

Kennedy, Senator Edward M. 89, **89**
Khe Sanh 10

Lam, Lieutenant General Hoang Xuan 22
Lam Son 216, Operation 10–11
Lan, Colonel Ma Vinh 23, 35
LeClair, Lieutenant Timothy 78
Life magazine 90
Lipscomb, Lieutenant Thomas 72
Littnan, Captain Charles 44–46, 50, 68

McGovern, Senator George S. 89
Massachusetts Striker, Operation **12**, 13
Merjil, Specialist Edward 80
Midway Conference 90
Military Assistance Command, Vietnam (MACV) 6, 24–25, 88, 91
Montgomery, Major Kenneth H. 47
Montgomery Rendezvous, Operation 13

napalm **44**, 50
Nelson, Specialist Phil 45
New York Times 70, 90
Nguyen, Kieu Tam 35
Nixon, President Richard M. 5–6, **6**, 90, 90–91
North Vietnamese Army (NVA) 6, 28–32, **30**
    plan for battle 34–36
    324th Div
        29th Regt 30–31, 44–46, 88
        806th Bn 54–55
    325th Div
        95th Regt 9
    816th Main Force Bn 11
    818th Main Force Bn 11
    K-12 Sapper Bn 52–53, 54, 55

People's Army of Vietnam (PAVN) *see* North Vietnamese Army (NVA)
People's Liberation Armed Forces (PLAF) *see* Viet Cong
Perron, Specialist Philip 71
Pink (helicopter) Teams 70
Project Delta patrols 10

Quan Doi Dang Dan see North Vietnamese Army (NVA)
Quan Doi Giai Phong Nhan Dan see Viet Cong

Rakkasans *see* US forces, 3/187th Regt
Rocklen, Private Michael 72
Rogers, William P. 76
Route 548: 7

Sanders, Captain Luther 59, 63–64, 72
Sharbutt, Jay 70, 89
Sherron, Lieutenant Colonel Gene 76–77
Shumaker, Lieutenant Ian 78
Skaggs, Private Paul 78–79
Smith, Brigadier General Jim 64
smoke marker 75

'Snake and Nape' bombing 61
Somerset Plain, Operation **11**, 11–12
Special Forces camp, attack on 9–10
Stilwell, Lieutenant General Richard G. 13, 17, **17**
Stymiest, Captain William 78
suicide attacks 79
Summers, Colonel Harry 91
support for the war 90

Tet Offensive, 1968: 5
Thieu, President Nguyen Van **90**, 91
Torba, Lieutenant Gerald 59
Trautman, Lieutenant Joel 59, 63, 74
Truong, Major General Ngo Quang 22, **22**, 76

US forces 24–27, 33–34
   III Marine Amphibious Force (MAF) 9
   101st Airborne Div (Airmobile) 25
     2nd Bde 13
     3/187th Regt 26, 38, 39–87
     2/327th Regt 11, 12
     2/501st Regt 13, 22, 38, 51, 52–53, 54, 55, 69, 77–80, 86
     1/502nd Regt 13, 22
     1/506th Regt 22, 38, 49, 55, 69, 73, 77–80, 86

2/506th Regt 76, 85–86
1st Cav Div (Airmobile) 10
2/17th Cav Regt 10
1st Marine Div
   1/9th Marine Regt 12, 22
   2/9th Marine Regt 22
11th Field Artillery 55
319th Field Artillery 55

Vallone, Specialist Michael 85
Viet Cong 28–30

Walden, Lieutenant Jerry 72
weapons
   NVA
     82mm mortar 32
     120mm mortar 32
     AK-47 rifle 52–53, 54
     free-flight rockets 32
     MON-100 Claymore mine 61, 72
     rocket-propelled grenade launcher 31, 52–53, 54
     RP-46 machine gun 31
     RPD machine gun 31
     SKS carbine 31
     Type 52 recoilless rifle 31, 32
     Type 53 mortar 31
     Type 54 DShK machine gun 31

US
   105mm howitzer **11**, 27, **52–53**, 54, 55
   107mm mortar 27
   155mm howitzer 27, 51, **52–53**, 54, 55
   BLU-82B Commando Vault 'Daisy Cutter' 34, **34**
   M2 mortar 28
   M16 rifle 26, 28, **82–83**, 84
   M18 recoilless rifle 28
   M29 mortar 28, **78**
   M60 machine gun 26, 28, **78**, **82**, 84
   M67 recoilless rifle 28
   M79 grenade launcher 26, 28, **62**
weather conditions 8–9, 12, 75
Westmoreland, General William C. 6
Wilson, Lieutenant Colonel Joseph C. 22
wire cutters **52–53**, 54
Wright, Major General John M. 18–19, 89

Young, Senator Stephen M. 89

Zais, Major General Melvin 17–18, **18**, 64, 75–76, 89